D1013431

Matter
into feeling

Matter into feeling

A new alchemy of science and spirit

Fred Alan Wolf, Ph.D.

Moment Point Press
Portsmouth, New Hampshire

FURTHER PRAISE FOR
MATTER INTO FEELING

Moment Point Press, Inc.
P.O. Box 4549
Portsmouth, NH 03802-4549
www.momentpoint.com

Matter into Feeling: A New Alchemy of Science and Spirit

Cover design by Metaglyph and Susan Ray
MG

Library of Congress Cataloging-in-Publication Data

Wolf, Fred Alan
  Matter into feeling : a new alchemy of science and spirit / Fred Alan Wolf, Ph.D.
    p. cm
  Includes bibliographical references and index.
  ISBN 1-930491-00-X (alk. paper)
    1. Mind and body.   2. Matter.   3. Emotions.   4. Philosophy.

BF161.W64 2002
110--dc21   2002005909

Printed in the United States of America

10 9 8 7 6 5 4 3 2 1

This book is printed on recycled acid-free paper.

Moment Point Press
Portsmouth, New Hampshire

To my mentor the late Carlo Suarès. His vision guides me.

Also to my wife, Sonia, who provides the necessary reflection of love in my life and the reminder that the One Mind can only be witnessed through another's eyes.

And I would like to thank Natalie Reid for a helpful discussion regarding Hebrew characters and words.

ALSO BY FRED ALAN WOLF

Mind into Matter
The Spiritual Universe
The Dreaming Universe
The Eagle's Quest
Parallel Universes
The Body Quantum
Star Wave
Taking the Quantum Leap
Space-Time and Beyond

Contents

Transforming Matter into Feeling

Shall we be able to realize, on a higher plane, alchemy's old dream of psychophysical unity, by the creation of a unified conceptual foundation for the scientific comprehension of the physical as well as the psychical?

Wolfgang Pauli, physicist

In my previous book, *Mind into Matter*, my goal was to show that within your own mind and body lies a majestic story filled with drama, pathos, humor, intelligence, fantasy, and fact. While it is certainly your own story, it is also the story of the entire universe, its creation, transformation, and ultimate purpose. I showed how this story called "you" unfolds into a panorama of life, literally a "you-niverse." I explored how the basic operations of what I call the *new alchemy*—thinking, sensing, feeling, and intuiting—form and shape the primary material of our conscious and unconscious life. And we saw that reshaping this primary material gives rise to forces that transform the world and us, namely creation, animation, resistance, vitality, replication, chance, unification, structure, and transformation. The ultimate goal of all this being the transmutation of information into matter; matter arises from mind—a vast field of influence commonly envisioned as the Mind of God.

You may consider *Mind into Matter*, then, to be an introduction into what the ancients called the "great work" of new alchemy. And now having introduced you to the new alchemy, much remains to be explored. We might ask ourselves, for example, How do I use the tools presented in *Mind into Matter* to change myself? How do I realize these transformational forces? How do I live a more creative and fruitful spiritual life?

Realization of the new alchemy brings novel forms of the creative transforming forces into play. While the mind-to-matter transformation deals with primary or archetypal images and how these images become material, the next phase of the great work is the transformation of the newly-formed matter into feeling. This is where we begin to feel life in our bodies, as real living tissue. And this applies to all living beings, as all living beings feel. Feeling goes beyond the senses and can be imagined as the fundamental awareness out of which all of the other senses develop. Feeling results from the incessant "hum" of life itself.

In *Mind into Matter* I brought forward the notion of *Adam Kadmon*—the universal and archetypal human. This Adam, unlike the original Adam of the Bible, is capable of realizing at once spirit, matter, and full powers of transformation. What makes Adam Kadmon differ from the biblical Adam can be summarized into one word: *feeling*. The Adam of the Book of Genesis seems almost an automaton, incapable of any real feeling, except perhaps for the feeling of shame when he and Eve are thrown out of Eden. Adam Kadmon, on the other hand, is capable of feeling deeply all of the transformational possibilities embedded within him. So we can say that Adam represented the first phase of the transformation—mind into matter—while Adam Kadmon represents the second phase—matter into feeling.

As with *Mind into Matter*, *Matter into Feeling* is divided into nine chapters, each framed by the nine letter-symbols of the Hebrew alphabet, or "aleph-bayt." In *Mind into Matter* we dealt with the archetypes spirit, represented by aleph (א, 1), through structure, represented by tayt (ט, 9). Now we will be concerned with their development—their transformation from seeds into young sprouts. This is accomplished in Qabala by multiplying each letter-symbol by the number ten. Since the letter-symbol for ten in Hebrew is *yod*, meaning existence, we see that multiplying by ten each of the nine archetype letter-symbols actualizes them, brings them into existence, or as I put it, brings matter into feeling.

Thus aleph (א), representing number 1, transforms into yod (י), number 10; bayt (ב, 2) becomes khaf (כ, 20); ghimel (ג, 3) becomes lammed (ל, 30); dallet (ד, 4) becomes mem (מ, 40); hay (ה, 5) becomes noon (נ, 50); vav (ו, 6) becomes sammekh (ס, 60); zayn (ז, 7) becomes ayn (ע, 70); hhayt (ח, 8) becomes phay (פ, 80); and tayt (ט, 9) becomes tsadde (צ, 90). In each chapter opening I will review these transformations and explain in more detail what they mean.

The advancement of the letter-symbols points to experience, life, reality, and so on, with the symbols coming alive, as it were. *Matter into Feeling*, then, looks at the continual movement of the nine mental/material seed archetypes into living symbols, literally a transformation of matter—already embodying mind—into life, the feeling and awareness of matter.

Note, too, that when we put two letter-symbols together, indicating a transformation from the former to the latter, they occasionally spell out a Hebrew word that symbolizes that transformation. In ancient Hebrew there may have been more examples of a matching between ancient words and the sacred meaning of the letters. Short of that, by going through a typical modern Hebrew/English dictionary I came up with words, shown below, that typify the transformation. In those cases where no word seemed to exist, I used the Qabala definition of the symbols:

aleph to yod (א to י; 1 to 10)
island—the movement to self-identity

bayt to khaf (ב to כ; 2 to 20)
birth—the movement from dream to reality

ghimel to lammed (ג to ל; 3 to 30)
wave—the movement from wave to feeling

dallet to mem (ד to מ; 4 to 40)
blood—the movement of the trickster

hay to noon (ה to נ; 5 to 50)
curve of life—the movement toward balance

vav to sammekh (ו to ס; 6 to 60)
menses—the movement of sexual energy

zayn to ayn (ז to ע; 7 to 70)
observation—the movement of the universe

hhayt to phay (ח to פ; 8 to 80)
purity—the movement from self to soul

tayt to tsadde (ט to צ; 9 to 90)
structure of love—the movement of life

In bringing mind into matter we had to deal with resistance and the trickster element. Now, similarly, we must deal with the conflicts and resistance we face in our lives as we attempt to make sense of the world, and learn to put up with our material demands, our addictions, our ups and downs, successes and failures. For many of us on the spiritual path, the great work gets trapped here—we live and die never realizing that other phases of transformation are even possible. In other words, we get fooled by our appetites.

To make the leap, to realize the remaining phases, requires understanding that the "stuck" life is only a phase, much as a child throwing a tantrum is merely "going through a phase." The movement of matter into feeling is the second phase. And my goal with *Matter into Feeling* is to help guide you through it.

aleph (א, 1)
to
yod (י, 10)

The Book of Genesis presents the timeless, metaphorical battle of matter with spirit—the continuing story of man acting against God. This story resonates through a number of biblical scenarios, including Adam and Eve's willful ignoring of God in the Garden of Eden, Abraham's sacrifice of Isaac, and God's refusing Moses entry into the new world.

The Hebrew alphabet provides letter-symbols of this war of matter with spirit: aleph, representing unembodied spirit, and yod, representing spirit contained and limited in matter that in its pride fights against the very thing that brought it into reality. And thus the transformation of aleph to yod is symbolized by the word island—*the movement to self-identity.*

CHAPTER 1

The Island of Feeling
We Call the Body

*No man is an island, entire of himself; every man is a
piece of the continent.*

John Donne

Much like Narcissus, who was punished by the goddess
Nemesis for resisting Echo's call,[1] spirit embedded in matter as
self—meaning body consciousness—resists spirit's call. In doing
so, embodied spirit makes a primary distinction: recognizing itself as matter, it becomes entranced, lost in the image of itself as
separate from spirit. An illusion, and a powerful one. Thus we, as
self, begin the lifelong process of distinguishing one thing from
another, a process from which we derive both joy and suffering.

The ability to carry out this action, to make objective
discriminations, constitutes scientific intelligence and remains necessary for material survival. The difference between
scientific intelligence and spiritual intelligence lies in this
ability to discern. It seems the two forms of experience produce a *complementarity*.

To explain, in quantum physics the principle of complementarity says that the physical universe can never be known
independent of an observer's choices of what to observe. More-
over, these choices fall into two distinct, or complementary, sets

of observations called *observables*. Observation of one observable always precludes the possibility of simultaneous observation of its complement. For example, the observation of the location and the observation of the motion of a subatomic particle form complementary observables. Hence the observation of one renders the other indeterminate or uncertain. So the more objective we are in our observations, the more difficulty we will have in dealing with spirit, and the more likely we will become drawn into the material world.[2] Conversely, as we become more spiritually awakened, the less concern we will feel for our material existence.

It's true, scientists have mastered the ability to find particles of matter standing alone with separate properties. Yet they witnessed every electron behaving exactly alike and each atom differing not a chemical whit from any other atom with the same atomic number. Hydrogen is hydrogen and copper is copper, wherever they may roam.[3] This principle of scientific identity seems to hold throughout the universe and indicates that matter only exists according to certain basic structural rules. So although matter appears as separate particles, the fact that they are identical particles tells us that their separation is illusory.

Scientists could have imagined all kinds of matter,[4] but something compelled them to find a simpler, rational basis for all that we experience as matter. That basis culminated into only perceiving matter objectively. With the discovery of quantum physics, however, science uncovered reality's own subjective nature; it found everything connected, joined in identity as if mirrored, and this, in the sense of identical particle construction, pointed to a unity of all matter. It also showed that a deeper, non-material reality played a significant role in determining how objective matter behaved.

But in spite of the compelling evidence of material unity and the recognition of matter's deeper, non-material basis, scientists, with a few notable exceptions,[5] still find spiritual concerns troubling. Thus the battle of spirit with its own reflection in matter goes on. And together matter and spirit make the world into a series of separate "islands." Each island appears to itself and sees the other islands as distinct. As each of us comes into the world, we begin to see ourselves as isolated beings, separate islands seemingly adrift in the vast ocean of life.

In this chapter, we will explore the nature of "island formation," how the individual islands we call our separate lives come into existence. We will learn how coming into feeling—bringing mind into the body—on the one hand gives us the experience we call life, and on the other hand provides each of us with a sense of loneliness and separation from all others. And we will learn to see, though perhaps only dimly, that we are still one. We may appear to ourselves as islands, but we form a continent of life.

THE EGO, STRESS, AND ITS RELIEF

Narcissus dies at the edge of the river gazing at his own reflection. Each of us suffers a similar malady as we gaze intently at the images we call our bodies. Unlike Narcissus, however, we don't just lie there, lost in our reflection. We move on, all the while feeling the loss as we miss the echo of our soul—our spirit calling to us. We live in continual stress arising from the anxiety of the ongoing battle between matter and spirit (body and soul). Some of you may object to this idea, claiming that through special techniques, meditation, spiritual practice, or simply being a good person, we may experience relief from this stress. But, like the suffering of Narcissus, the stress I refer to *must* continually arise from spirit and body opposing each other. The battle results in a continual conflict we all feel as our common human suffering. Ironically, it is this very condition that makes life worthwhile and leads to the wonderful drama of our daily reality.

Our human condition depends on the rise of spiritual stress. And here the mind enters the game. More than any other causative factor, our thoughts amplify this stress. More important than any medical care, good mental habits promote relief from this stress amplification. By good mental habits I mean simply thinking positively about every situation we encounter, even when critical thought is required.

And while human existence is dependent upon human thought, thought is dependent on our self-concepts—our egos. Sigmund Freud gave us our basic concept of the *ego*. But Freud was so involved with materialism, in scientifically proving the ego's existence as something real, he got caught in science's objectivity trap. Since then, the concept of the ego has undergone many revisions. The ideas of Freud, along with the more recent ideas of spiritual teachers such as Da Free John,[6] J. Krishnamurti, Paramahansa Yogananda, and the disincarnate entity Seth, have provided me with an insight into the quantum physics of the construction of the ego.

The Freudian Ego

Freud saw the ego as a construction within the psyche (or soul)[7] that arose out of a previous psychic construct he called the *id*. He envisioned the id as being the oldest psychical apparatus, an idea that arose from his basic assumption that every human being has an inner mental life that comes about through a *psychical apparatus*. This apparatus, Freud believed, materially exists, possessing both spatial and temporal extent. Freud never hinted as to where the id exists or from what it is constructed. He only said that the id "contains everything that is inherited, that is present at birth, that is laid down in the constitution—above all, therefore, the instincts, which originate from the somatic organization and which find a first psychical expression here [in the id] in forms unknown to us."[8]

In materialistic terms, Freud saw the id and ego as follows: The ego arises out of the id, because the id must interface with the "real" world of stimulation and sensation. That portion of the id called the ego undergoes a special transformation. From the surface of the brain cortex itself—that is, a cortical layer—a special organization arises which acts as the intermediary zone between the id and the outside world's stimulation. The ego, in consequence of the preestablished connection between sense perceptions and muscular action, has voluntary movement at its command. It has the task of self-preservation, a task that it can perform by becoming aware of stimulation, by avoidance of stimulation, by memory, by adaptation, and by learning. It operates within the id by gaining control over the id's demands (the instincts), by choosing which demands to satisfy, by postponing the id's satisfactions, and by consideration of tensions produced by stimuli. Further, the ego is able to differentiate between these tensions in terms of what is felt as pain (non-pleasure) and pleasure. The actual sensing of pleasure exists as a vibrational pattern between two poles of tension called the pain and pleasure points. An increase in tension is felt as pain, a decrease is felt as pleasure. In his theory of the instincts, Freud put forth that the main tensions arose not between the points of pain and pleasure, but between two basic instincts: love and death.

We owe much to the genius of Freud. Since his time, ego has become a major word in Western vocabulary and a point of much consideration for the rational human. Today, however, we see that ego arises as a spirit/matter interface. Let's look at some of the more recent ideas concerning ego.

The Spiritual Ego

Da Free John considers the Freudian ego to be a devastating construct that keeps human beings from realizing their god-selves.[9] He points out that we each live in *egoic stress*. The ego, he says, is a process of self-possessed physical, emotional, and mental reaction to the circumstances of life—the ego's action is stress production. And stress, he explains, is easy to trigger through either the frustration of self-motion or through the fear of taking that motion. The stress, therefore, is released by either making the motion or by relaxing and releasing the frustration reaction.

In order to accomplish this release, one must learn to notice when stress is arising, a major insight gained through self-knowledge. Sounds simple enough, but few of us actually notice when we are becoming stressed. In fact, noticing that we are stressed and at the same time feeling the stress is like the proverbial rub-your-stomach-pat-your-head trick. In a typical situation, someone may say something to you that is particularly upsetting. You might react by getting angry or feeling depressed. Although you are certainly aware of how you feel, you normally aren't aware that a stress has arisen as a result of these feelings. In other words, you feel, but you don't know you feel.

For example, we have all witnessed, at one time or another, a person who is obviously angry but who answers "no" when asked if he is feeling angry. On first impression, we might think the person is lying. He *must* see that he is angry, we say to ourselves, why can't he "tell the truth." But from where you stand, you have some objectivity—something the angry person does not have. Remember, knowledge of a feeling and the feeling itself are complementary to each other.[10] The knowledge that you are having a feeling will alter that feeling.

Paramahansa Yogananda describes the ego as the root cause of dualism—the seeming separation between man and his creator.[11] According to Yogananda , *ahankara* (desire) brings human beings under the sway of *maya* (cosmic delusion), by which the subject (ego) falsely appears as object.

J. Krishnamurti suggests that our brains, when looked at collectively, are very old. A human brain is not any particular brain; it doesn't belong to anyone. It, instead, has evolved over millions of years. Consequently, there are built-in patterns for success and survival that exist today, but that may be outmoded. One of these patterns is the ego and its tendencies.[12]

The disincarnate entity Seth describes the ego as specialized in expansions of space and its manipulations.[13] The ego arose in tribal environments as a necessary specialization; it enabled data from the senses to be differentiated emotionally and otherwise. Tribes formed in which members were considered as being either inside or outside the tribe. This tribal consciousness was the first group ego. Later, as group consciousness waned due to adaptive evolutionary increase in individual awareness, consciousness was not able to handle the tribal ego as it was, and individuation began to take place.

A QUANTUM-PHYSICAL MODEL OF THE EGO

So what do these definitions of ego all add up to? We need to recognize that the ego is dynamic—it changes depending on the feelings a person has. We are all familiar with the terms "crushed ego" and "big ego." Based on such common sense terms, we might say that if a person feels *expansive* the ego actually expands and the person feels a sense of exaltation. I'll explain this in more detail further on, but note here that I don't mean the ego inflates in the Jungian sense of *inflation*, meaning puff up with pride. Indeed most likely Jungian inflation results from a blow to the ego resulting, paradoxically, in its contraction. If a person feels contained, the ego undergoes a contraction, possibly a depression or feeling of humility or compassion.

I would like to expand (pun intended) on this metaphorical picture of the ego by introducing a model based on quantum physics. Quantum physics deals with mathematical imaginal forms that represent physical possibilities in the real world. This quantum physics model represents mental forms that represent psychological possibilities we may feel when our egos are involved in any life transaction.

Just as quantum physical models determine and represent the stability and energetic behavior of matter, this model will determine and represent the stability and feeling behavior of mind. I believe this suggests that the ego appears real, not physical—it is not a material object but a construct of mind. Thus the ideal place to find the ego would be in the imaginal realm, the mathematical world of quantum physics. Here the ego appears as a closed surface, like the surface of a sphere or the six sides of a cube. In general, any object enclosed within a boundary will possess an ego.[14]

Particles Have Egos

Many physicists believe that all matter is composed of trapped light,[15] a belief embodied in Einstein's famous $E=mc^2$. According to this equation, when matter emits light energy, it loses some of itself—its mass diminishes. Thus, matter is imagined to be trapped light.

In one of my earlier books, *Star Wave*, I speculate that human feelings such as love and hate could be described in terms of simpler and more primitive base feelings found in the matter-light transformations of electrons.[16] For example, hate (which I take to be synonymous with desire for isolation), is connected with the fact that no two electrons will ever exist in the same quantum state. Love is explained in terms of the behavior of light particles—photons. All photons tend to move into the same state if given the chance; thus, in a physical sense, the phrase "light is love" is no exaggeration. Hence love represents people tending to be in a unified state of consciousness, as in, for example, lovers being of like minds, or becoming one with God.

In a similar sense, we all suffer from loneliness and other pain connected with our material bodies because of this isolation—or hate—property of electrons. Electrons composed of trapped light desire freedom. Electrons "feel" some form of suffering because of this confinement.[17] Our human suffering arises from theirs and comes out of a desire to become light once again. All of our human feelings and emotions are rooted in these simple physical properties of matter. Or perhaps better put, in light of the new alchemy spirit, the physical properties of matter and the feeling properties we experience come from a deeper place where mind and matter are not separate.

The Quantum Id and Its Feelings

As we saw above, the id is the womb of the ego. Since the id, according to Freud, is composed of timeless states, these states accompany the energy states of the complex human-energy system.[18] Out of the id arise emotions that cause the body to move and give rise to sensations. That means energy states and emotional states are one and the same in the body. Thus, when feeling expresses itself, energy transforms— changes from one form to another, as when you get up from a chair and transform the potential chemical energy of the body into kinetic or motion energy.

Not everything expressed energetically, however, is sensed. What we call the sensation of feeling arises from transformation of energy, and this transformation requires a rather complex neural network.

Perhaps it would be useful to emphasize that *feelings* and *sensations* are not the same thing. I'm using these terms as Carl Jung did. Sensations involve movements of electrons or other electrically charged particles from one place to another—as, for example, in the nervous system or in the brain or muscles. A sensation implies the existence of a disturbing event, such as a pin prick on skin or a grain of sugar melting on a taste bud. Sensations include vibration, heat, cold, taste, smell, sight, and sound.[19] For a sensation to arise, some location in the body must register it. Sensations occur when some particle interacts with a registering device in the body, usually a nerve ending in the skin or, in the case of sight, the retina of the eye. The skin registers a pin prick, for example, while the tongue registers a taste.

Feelings, on the other hand, correspond to a thoughtless (not in the pejorative sense, but literally, as in *no thought occurring*) evaluation of sensation. For instance, we may consider a particular vibration as a "good vibe" when it comes from a loving friend, or as a "bad vibe" when it comes from someone hostile. We might feel elation upon tasting great food or comfort upon feeling a warm fire on our cold skin. And while feelings involve sensations, they are not dependent on them. In dreams or in remembrances, for example, we can have feelings without sensations causing them. In my new alchemy, feelings give rise to waves, whereas sensations correspond to particles.

Further, feelings would not be sensed if nerve cells did not have membrane boundaries. Feelings produce electrical changes in the boundaries of nerve cells, which in turn cause bodily sensations. Thus, "felt" feelings are feelings transformed into sensations. In other words, when feelings are felt or expressed, the body experiences sensations.

Strong feelings lead to indeterminate sensations, as, for example, when people laugh at funerals because their sense of loss is so strong. In a similar manner, strong sensations lead to indeterminate feelings about them—think, for example, about how you felt when you first tasted a jalapeño pepper. On the other hand, you can experience certain feelings and sensations simultaneously with no difficulty. You can feel joy, for instance, when holding a newborn child in your arms. More than likely, this ability or inability comes through the complementarity principle as it pertains to the feeling wave and particle location at nerve endings where a sensation arises. So certain combinations of feeling and sensation can be experienced simultaneously, while others cannot. What works and what doesn't depends, to a large extent, on you and the shape of your ego.

The ego emerges from energy transformations expressed as bodily sensations. Therefore, the ego does not simply exist in the brain, it exists as a memory that indicates wherever cells have boundaries and whenever those boundaries undergo spatial change. In a sense, every cell has an ego. Any living entity that has a surface, in fact, will have an ego. Animals have egos, and so do plants, amoebas, and other single-celled forms of life. To grasp how the ego arises and undergoes change or transformation, we need to take a closer look at a concept I mentioned earlier in this chapter, the observer effect—the most important factor of quantum physics.

The Observer Effect

According to the observer effect, the act of observation is always accompanied by a sudden, irreversible leap in the thing observed. When an atom's light strikes the eye and its energy is measured, the atom, having existed previously in a timeless state of "no energy"—or, in other words, as a superposition of all possible energy states with equal probabilities—suddenly expels a specific energy state when the light photon is emitted. This sudden expulsion comes from a discontinuous quantum leap from one state to another. No physical law determines which specific energy will be emitted. The fact remains that in some way we, as observers, determine this. For example, these quantum leaps can occur in complementarily differing ways, depending on how one expects to observe them—what instruments one uses. Here we see how the quantum physical law of complementarity works to shape the ways and means of our daily life by shaping the atoms that interact with us.

In the complementarity of the new alchemy, every thought comprises a wide range of potentially possible feelings, and every feeling comprises a wide range of potential thoughts. The energy state of "feeling good," for example, is composed of complementary thought states. These thoughts include both "I feel good" and "I feel lousy." Thus, when you begin to question your feelings, which means bringing into power the apparatus for thinking instead of the complementary apparatus for feeling, you have "mixed feelings" about how good you actually feel.

For example, while you make love and your bodily sensations transform into feelings, you rarely think about it. And by not thinking, you experience sublime feelings; indeed, that's what lovemaking is all about. But the moment you begin to think to yourself, "I wish my partner would do this," or, "I wish that I felt that," your sensations continue, but your feelings are changed completely. Or, consider another example. Imagine you are listening to a charismatic speaker. If the speaker's manner is "sexy" or "warm," you may find yourself "swept away" by the words, even though if you dispassionately read on paper those same words, you might find them disagreeable. Your feelings are aroused by the speaker, and your logical ability to follow the contents of the speaker's words is diminished. As the old Yiddish saying goes, "When the penis awakens, the brain falls asleep." Through just such complementary devices, dictators have come to power.

Thinking and feeling are complementary. So are sensing and intuiting. Intuiting depends on bodily sensations and is complementary to them in the same manner that feelings depend on thoughts. That hair prickling on the back of your neck is the sensation arising from the intuition that someone is behind you, or that something is likely to occur in the near future. When the "psychical apparatus" chosen is "thoughtful," feelings are altered and often indefinable. So too, when that apparatus is "feeling," thoughts are altered and often indefinable. Every observation comes from choices you make associated with indeterminate feelings when thoughts arise and, conversely, associated with indeterminate thoughts when feelings arise.

Thus, associated with every observation there will be a complementary observation. The apparatus that causes these choices to be made lies within and is constructed from the id. It is the ego, and here is how it arises.

THE RISE AND CREATION OF THE EGO, STRESS, AND PAIN

The province of the ego is the body-mind. The body-mind defines the boundary between the body and the mind. If we look at this boundary carefully, it blurs, and the distinction between the body and the mind vanishes.

"The unenlightened body-mind," according to Da Free John, "is founded on the actions of self-contraction. The self-contraction is expressed as the differentiation of self from the *Transcendental Source-Condition* and from every other form of presumed not-self, and is likewise expressed via the independent definition of self and the constant concern and search for independent self-preservation. The self-based or self-contracting and self-preserving conception of existence is manifested via the psychology of fear and conflict relative to all that is not-self."[20]

Yogananda describes the various links between normal mental modifications and functions in the Sankhya and Yoga systems. He states, "The different sensory stimuli to which we react: tactual, visual, gustatory, auditory, and olfactory, are produced by vibratory variations in electrons and protons."[21] These depend, in turn, on what is called the *maya* of duality—maya meaning, literally, "cosmic illusion" and also "the measurer." Thus, maya is the magical power in creation by which limitations and divisions apparently are present in the Immeasurable and the Inseparable.

Both Da Free John and Yogananda point to the separation that arises between "self" and "not-self." This separation manifests in everyone's own consciousness. During a quiet time, when you have managed to reduce distractions to a minimum, try to become aware of the self that is aware of the common senses you experience. For example, close your eyes for a brief moment and watch as thoughts arise in your mind. Pay them no heed, just let them pass by and simply become aware that you are having thoughts. As you continue this process, pay attention to the process of thinking. You will become aware of the division between thinking and the thinker—the self (or thinker) and the not-self (thoughts).

Once each of us identifies with our thoughts, sensations, feelings, and intuitions, we begin to play maya's game. By returning to the timeless, thoughtless, feelingless, and intuitionless state, we cease playing the game, but nevertheless *live*.

Egocentric existence is thus founded on a fundamental illusion that each and every being will exist forever and separately for all time. This illusion causes all kinds of misfortune involving control of being, existence, and the lives of others. It also causes fear, sorrow, and anger simply because at its heart lies a fundamental error.

The Model

The model I propose here, based on the observer's effect upon any quantum-physically confined particle, group of particles, cell, or neuron, applies at the human level.

Consider an object, otherwise completely free of interaction with any other thing, confined to move within a certain space. In quantum physics, such a system is called "a particle in a box" (see figure 1.1). According to quantum physics the "particle" will no

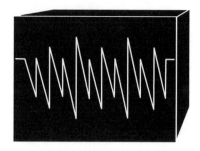

Figure 1.1. Electron in a Box. It looks like a wave.

longer look like a particle, but instead will spread itself out in the shape of a wave. The particle, because it is confined, will not be able to exist outside the volume of the box. Each time it reaches a boundary wall, speaking in classical physics terms, it bounces off and returns to the confines of the enclosed box.

In the language of new physics, the particle never possesses a well-defined location inside the box. According to the uncertainty principle,[22] a precise location would provide it with an enormous uncertainty in momentum or energy, likely resulting in its escaping from the box with explosive energy. Instead of dealing with the particle's certain position at each instant of time, in quantum physics we talk about the particle's *probability wave* that vanishes at the box's boundaries (again, see figure 1.1). This means that the probability of locating the particle at or on the boundary is zero.

The box's walls act on the wave in much the same manner that fingers, pegs, or struts act on a plucked guitar string. The pegs hold the string down, keeping the pegged portions of the string from vibrating, which allows only certain musical notes on the string.

According to quantum physics, the object behaves just like a bounded string. Only certain energy states for the boxed object can ever be experienced, just as only certain notes can be heard on a fixed length of guitar string. Consequently, because of the boundary conditions, the object's energy will only exist in certain states, just as harmonics exist on plucked string. When a guitar or violin player places his finger so that the vibrating portion of the string is shortened, the tone of the vibrating string rises. Likewise, lengthening the vibrating portion of the string lowers the tone. So a bass fiddle, for example, has a lower pitch than a violin because it has a longer vibrating string.

Similarly, in quantum physics, if the boundaries of the box are moved farther apart, increasing the box's volume, the wave spreads out and produces a lower energy (see figure 1.2). If the box's boundaries move closer together, decreasing the volume, the wave contracts and produces a higher energy (see figure 1.3). In other words, higher energy is produced in a smaller box; lower energy in a larger box.

It takes more energy to produce energy changes in a small box than a large box. An electron free to roam a box as big as a room would continually undergo minuscule energy changes, but an electron confined to an atom would only undergo much larger energy changes, as with violin notes. Hence small boxed particles are more stable or resistant to change than larger boxed particles. Particles in large boxes may undergo continual

Figure 1.2. Electron in a Wider Box. The wave spreads out and the energy lowers.

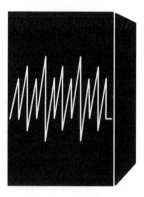

Figure 1.3. Electron in a Narrower Box. The
wave contracts and the energy rises.

changes, but they are smooth and gradual, much like the changes in tones heard on a bass fiddle. Particles in smaller boxes change energy in large measures, requiring nearly as much energy in the change as the particle possesses in the box. Changes in pitch on a bass fiddle, for example, are much harder to discern than changes in pitch on a violin because the difference in pitch between a bass's low notes is much smaller than the changes in pitch between the higher notes of a violin. Thus when we listen to Rimsky-Korsakov's "Flight of a Bumblebee" on a violin, we can hear clearly the rapid changes in the notes. Played on a bass fiddle, the notes are harder to discern.

The ego behaves in much the same manner as a box containing a bound particle. Let me explain this using a child's learning as an example. At first, as a child is forming in the womb with primary sense impressions, the ego boundary is quite large; no differentiation is made between the boundaries of the ego and the boundaries of the whole universe. The growing fetus, for example, does not differentiate itself from the womb that surrounds it. He or she is all-knowing, but unknowing that he or she is a child. Eventually events are imposed upon the sensory apparatus associated with pain or pleasure. For example, the mother may sing or hum a tune. The rhythmic vibrations of the mother's voice will most likely produce a soothing feeling in the child leading to his association of music with pleasure. Or the mother may receive upsetting news that causes her stress. This stress may affect the child in the womb so that the child feels undue discomfort and in adulthood may find himself overreacting to stressful situations, perhaps behaving irrationally. These acts form the child's ego.

In my simplified model of this formation, the original ego state—the ego you had before you were born—exists in a stable, bounded, but quite large space—the whole universe. But the first experiences quickly diminish your ego down to immediate surroundings. In this new space—the space of the womb—energy levels are still close together and transformations between them take place rapidly, resulting in sensory experience. The world of the child has been separated into a knowing and a known, a self and a not-self.

The actions of the ego, then, are similar to the actions of the particle in the box. When a learning experience occurs, the ego contracts in the same way that the boundaries of the box contract. This contraction can occur in two ways: either

1. The newly formed box precisely contains the wave it held, with no change in form, energy, or pitch. I label this as *rational contraction.* Or,
2. An energy change occurs because the wave changes its form in order to fit the new box. I label this as *irrational contraction.*

Let me return to the mother and fetus example I gave earlier.

Example 1: As a fetus hears mom's music in the womb, the most likely contractions of the ego would be rational simply because music itself requires rational notes such as the notes played on a violin string. The child's music memory would emulate these notes and the child should have a better appreciation for music than a child born in a less musical environment.

Example 2: On the other hand there are many irritating noises, such as those produced in a noisy neighborhood, which could affect the mother and the growing fetus. Although I can't prove this scientifically, I would suggest that children born in a noisy environment would tend to overreact to noise, either experiencing physical stress or expending much energy to avoid such stress. Perhaps this provides some insight into the apparent need of some youth to indulge in loud music.

In example 1, the egoic rational contraction reproduces an unblemished and pleasurable experience of the world. It contains a representation of the experience in much the same way that a miniature object represents the original object. In other words, it now holds a fairly fixed early memory. In example 2, the irrationally contracted ego experiences a trauma; there will be a memory associated with the new state, but it won't be a pleasant one.

In both examples 1 and 2, since the box has smaller boundaries, it becomes harder to induce changes in the energy (because contracted boxes are more stable than expanded boxes). But that means, analogously, that it is difficult to change the contracted ego by energetic means, such as physical activity. Hence we have persistent early memories that shape our egos into the people we eventually become.

If the ego could expand, it would tend to disrupt the memory pattern, much as an expanded box disrupts the energy states of a smaller box by lowering the pitch. The ego expansion will break the pattern, making it possible to learn again when a new contraction occurs. Tension, or the feeling of forces, arises when either expansions or contractions take place. In the box example, tension is a physical force on the particle; with the ego analogy, it is the feeling of mounting stress, or the release of that stress.

With rational contraction, no spikes of tension occur; indeed, there is nothing to even recall that a change has occurred.[23] The ego forms without any real awareness that it has taken form. With irrational contraction the ego attempts to modify or change by either further contraction or expansion. Mind you, I don't mean ego inflation as in the Jungian sense; I mean egoic expansion in the physical sense that the particle now attempts to occupy a larger space than it had previously.

Depending on the size of the contraction, it takes work, an expenditure of energy, to change a memory. The price of continual egoic contraction is apparent. Maintaining a small size takes more work for the cellular structure to undergo the changes in feeling that result in new memories. Rarely will these produce rational contractions. The usual situation will produce more irrational contractions simply because there are more irrational possibilities than rational ones.[24] This explains the difficulty we all have with life. No one escapes or enters life without suffering.

However, this doesn't mean that pleasurable memories are not possible as we age from adulthood to senior citizen status. Pleasant memories can be had by arranging to experience pleasant feelings in association with them. For example, it may be useful to have music in the background when attempting to solve a difficult problem or remember a new piece of data. When I need a break from writing, for example, I like to watch old movies. I feel a definite nostalgia whenever I watch them, most likely because they are associated with feelings of excitement that I experienced when I first saw them many years ago as a teenager or young man.

THE PHYSICS OF EGO EXPANSION, STRESS RELEASE, AND PLEASURE

Continual irrational contraction cannot result in anything more than pain or ennui. As we see in my simple model, irrational contraction can lead only to negative emotions associated with pain, such as sorrow, anger, and all kinds of destructive acts. And yet self-contraction appears to be a primal drive associated with survival as separate selves.

Contraction records memory. By making each egoic cell smaller, the world becomes larger and unfriendly. Each unit, in diminishing itself, actually programs itself for self-annihilation, much like the main character in the movie "The Incredible Shrinking Man." Yet we humans persist in this behavior under the illusion that "survival of the fittest" means survival of the individual. Remember, with ego shrinkage it takes more work to fuel new memories. Yet today shrinking egoic existence down to the size of atoms becomes the desired goal of our materialistic self-serving egoic existence.

But what can we do about contraction? According to quantum physics, we need to expand. What happens when a particle in a box finds itself in more space in which to wander? Here we see only one effect—the release of tension that can be felt as pleasure, possibly as pain, and even more possibly as enlightenment.

Expansion is, however, not just the opposite of contraction. It does not appear like a movie of a contraction run backward. Expansion results in tension-free existence. Yes, forces will always arise when the quantum physical system undergoes an expansion of its boundaries. The previously confined wave, upon expansion, finds itself in a larger space, and, like a wave, it sloshes back and forth in that space, attempting to reach an equilibrium it never finds.

I believe that these expansion forces give rise to ego release, to physical pleasure, simply because they are vibratory tensions or rolling sensations similar to what you experience in massage therapy when you let go of a tense muscle.

This difference between expansion and contraction constitutes the distinction between pleasure and pain. Pleasure arises from a continuous or smooth expansion. So, the closer the wave pattern resembles a smooth wave, the greater the pleasure.

Spikes of tension, on the other hand, which always occur under irrational contraction, cause too much change in the cell over too short a time period, the result being pain or anger. With changes in boundaries, the ego senses changes between pleasure and pain.

THE BODY'S QUANTUM EGO:
THE ISLAND OF FEELING

While no man is an island, island formation must occur in order for memory to exist. Your body is a large memory bank whose cellular surfaces form the egoic structures that enable you to deal with the wave of life. Your ego boundary dances with the wave attempting to catch it and surf it to the end. We have seen how quantum physics can be used to model this process. The ego's construction affects and forms our brains and nervous systems similar to the way in which energy forms the quantum world of a particle in a box. According to Freud, our brains possess psychical apparatuses, but he does not reveal what these apparatuses might be. Specifically, he doesn't tell us how our id and our ego are constructed.

Here I propose that the id is composed of many different feeling states of the psychical apparatus operating in the nervous system, in the same manner that energy states operating in the nervous system compose its physical states. The ego arises out of the id as a psychical operation, tending to choose which physical states are to be observed and remembered. The ego, then, consists of a complex network of quantum-physical imaginal surfaces in the body, resembling a matrix of three-dimensional boxes like a crystal lattice. (Any relevant closed surfaces will do here. I used boxes simply as an example.) The ego operates through contraction and expansion of these surfaces. Rational contraction reproduces pleasurable physical experience-memories, irrational contraction results in painful recall. Ego expansion, which means physical expansion of the closed surfaces, results in pleasure. Thus, the ego is limited by pain and pleasure and operates by expansion and contraction. Relief of stress comes with pleasure and, therefore, with an expansion of these closed boundaries. A similar expansion takes place in all the cells of the body when stress is relieved.

And next we will see the creativity of the ego's dance in the wave.

bayt (ב, 2)

to

khaf (כ, 20)

Bayt represents any container, any physical support, any gestalt. It is the first or primary divisor or separator, for to contain or hold is to separate that which is held from that which is not. It is the primary act, therefore, of consciousness recognizing itself by dividing itself.

Bayt transforms into khaf whenever an idea turns into something organically tangible. As bayt it remains seed-like, only a beginning of a form of limitation—a separation of one thing from another. As khaf, the creative vision becomes something literal that we can hold in our hand or reach out and touch. Khaf in Hebrew means palm of the hand.

CHAPTER 2

From a Dream to Reality

If you want to make an apple pie from scratch, you must first create the universe.

Carl Sagan

The most profound creative act we experience as humans beings is giving birth to our children. Great forces drive us to follow the commandment to reproduce. True, some of us hardly feel this primal urge, but it is there as the drive to ensure our future existence. We label it and commonly experience it as the sex drive. But this drive goes far beyond the survival of humankind, indeed it goes beyond the survival of all kinds of life. It continually bubbles up in each of us; it drives our existence by producing the ideas that flow through our heads, by forming the very words we speak.

Every living thing feels this drive to create. Your dog feels it. The snake in the grass feels it. The cells of your body feel it. Bugs feel it. And plants do, too. The constant flux of on/off, life/death, beginning/ending, that impossible presence of aleph—unembodied spirit—pulsates in each of us as bayt—consciousness recognizing itself. In this creative sense, we are all children of the vast mind-spirit that fills the universe and gave birth to it. And like our creator-spirit, each of us has the power to create. The evidence of this? We can think and speak.

Here we face the miracle of the creative action—our offspring. And these offspring may take the form of our own flesh and blood or the thoughts that spring from our foreheads, as in the myth of Zeus giving birth to his daughter Athena.[1] In this chapter, we will explore the alchemical underpinnings of the creative impulse—the feeling or urge to create—and the importance of the concept of the firstborn creation. We will see how creation implies and produces the living feeling we all experience. And we will see that like the Indian creator Brahma who dreams to create worlds, and the Australian aboriginal Great Spirit who dreams all of us into existence, we, too, find the source of our creative ability in our dreams.

It All Began as a Dream

In dreaming, we dreamers create a story or a play. Storytelling or playacting appear to be a very important part of human evolution; we dream because we need to dream in order to evolve. And, in fact, most creatures dream.[2]

Dreaming is the result of each creature's evolving awareness of how to adapt to its environment. If we looked at dreaming from a purely routine scientific point of view, we would have to say that dreams are important in that they allow creatures to develop strategies for survival or to alter programming from day-to-day environmental changes that occur. There is no simple way of defining what dreams are, but the current evidence indicates that they do play an evolutionary role.[3]

Darwinian evolution theory proclaims the evolution of life as a process of natural selection. Life, Darwin suggested, is a competitive struggle to survive, often in the face of limited resources. Living things must compete for food and space and evade predators and disease while dealing with unpredictable shifts in their environment. Darwin suggested that within a given population, within a given environment, certain individuals possess characteristics that make them more likely to survive and reproduce. Just how they come to acquire these characteristics remains a mystery, but they are passed on to offspring, nonetheless. If the acquired characteristic benefits the organism, the number of organisms with these new traits increases as each generation passes on the advantageous combination of traits. Conversely, individuals lacking the beneficial traits gradually decrease in number. Thus, Darwin argued, over time natural selection tips a population's balance toward those individuals with the combination of traits, or adaptations, best suited to their environment.[4]

But my question remains: Just how does a species acquire the needed characteristic? The dream experiences of Australian aboriginal peoples indicate that the needed characteristic arises, is first born, in dreams. Each creature dreams of the possibility for the next evolution, so that, for example, the fish dreams of the amphibian and the amphibian dreams of the bird, and so on. That is, we first dream in order to become aware of our future possibilities—the new ways that each one of us may exist. And that ability to sense oneself as something new or altered seems to be vital for survival, for altering the genetic code. If we lack this ability, we are not able to do as well as a species.

Furthermore, the ability to see future possibilities brings the future into the present. This future-to-present movement differs, of course, from the normal model in which we see time flowing in a linear fashion from past to present to future. Simply put, consciousness may work differently in the dream state than in our waking state.

Matter Dreams

Following modern science, if we believe that all consciousness arises from matter, matter itself must dream. We know dreams occur and that nearly all things dream. So, when

I say, matter dreams, I am simply following a logical line of thought based on materialist philosophy.

The argument goes like this: The universe is made of matter, and matter interacting with matter creates all the different physical phenomena that can be observed, including life and its evolutionary ways and mind. Life and consciousness are ultimately physical phenomena that can be observed. So anything that is associated with life must be associated with material objects banging together—interacting. Thus it must be that the dream state and all conscious awareness arise from interacting matter. And so, we draw the conclusion that matter dreams. Or so goes the logical conclusion of the materialist point of view.

That view, however, is not the conclusion I've come to, as I believe that materialism itself is flawed as a basis for understanding science; it's overly reductionistic. And I don't mind the reductionism so much as I mind the base on which the reductionism stands—that matter *is* the base. As I explained in *Mind into Matter*, I believe that matter must be a secondary quality, that there must be a more primal quality from which matter arises. In the same sense that there must be an implicate order, as physicist David Bohm would say, out of which consciousness and awareness arise, one would also say that there must be some order, which is not directly perceivable, out of which matter and space and time arise.[5]

We know—or let's say that we have experimental evidence that suggests—that there was a Big Bang, that the universe was created from a point. The theory is based upon two or three bits of very strong evidence. It doesn't necessarily mean that this is what happened absolutely, but it is what we currently believe based upon the evidence—that the universe came into being out of nothing.

And not only did it come into being, but all matter, space, and time also, simultaneously, came into being. From the general theory of relativity, matter didn't simply arise in space and time. It couldn't. Space and time had to arise *simul-*

taneously with matter and energy. And so matter can't be fundamental, and our materialist philosophy is flawed simply because it doesn't take into consideration the elemental concept of the Big Bang. There has to be something more fundamental than matter itself.

I'll offer one more thought that will help us in the next chapter. According to the quantum physics principle of complementarity, matter and energy turn out to be necessary complements to space and time. This means that we cannot describe the world of events in terms of space and time and in terms of energy and matter simultaneously. This turns out to be a deep clue pointing to the *as above so below, as within so without* axiom of the new alchemy. This complementarity, in fact, is just what we need to see if evolution is at all to resemble Darwin's view, or any other neo-form it might take.

WHAT'S MORE FUNDAMENTAL?

We can envision the fundamental ground of being out of which space, time, energy, and matter first appeared as the great mother-goddess or as the great father-god. These images appear again and again in ancient texts from many cultures.[6] Whatever else I might say about it would be my own viewpoint. So here it is.

There are several clues as to the existence of a more fundamental ground of being. One of the clues is the reality of the vacuum of space. We know that "empty" space itself can explode into matter and energy. And it can also envelope what it has created; it can reabsorb what it engendered. So you might say that the vacuum of space is capable of creation and annihilation wherein we have a continual dance of objects appearing and disappearing, rapidly, everywhere, all the time. This dance pervades all things and its result is that nothing is ever repeated exactly the same way, though it may appear so.

When space is absolutely void, when there is nothing, the process seems to be unstable, and there is a great tendency to produce objects. Once in a while the tendency even enables universes to "pop" into existence. The space *within* a universe, however, when it has already been created, seems to be more stable, relatively speaking, in terms of time; there seems to be less universe-making going on within a space-time universe. And once matter, space-time, and energy arise, there seems to be less tendency to produce another universe soon after, or in the immediate vicinity. Apparently, then, there is some rule as to how a universe should or should not be created.

From the "story" I just told, which is based on physics and speculation, there comes another story from spirituality, the Dance of Shiva. In this story, Shiva and Shakti dance the dance of creation and annihilation. Shiva is the Creator-Destroyer. Sometimes Shiva is presented as Shakti, the feminine consort of Shiva. He/she is the one who appears as Kali, the Goddess who kills and destroys in order for re-creation to occur. So the Dance of Annihilation and Creation, which is a part of modern physics, is also a part of ancient mythology.

And in the Qabala, the principles of ancient Judeo-Christian mysticism, which goes back to the time before there were Jews or Christians to the people from the land of Ur (now known as Iraq) there was a vision of this process going on. Spirit, symbolized by the letter aleph, the "firstborn" letter of the Hebrew alphabet, was capable of producing or emanating a vibrational movement in resistance to itself which was called water, or mem (the thirteenth letter of the Hebrew alphabet). Then spirit was able to breathe life into that water, and in so doing, there was a movement from the spirit into the water and from the water back into the spirit. This double-flowing movement was reminiscent of both the annihilation and creation process as well as the cycle of life and death.

The flow from the spirit to the water is creative; the flow from the water back to the spirit is destructive, producing a continual dance of life. This double-flow process can also symbolize the dance of awareness or consciousness, or even the movement of quantum waves of possibility from a present event to a future event, and then backward in time to the present event again.

So there are a number of analogies, hints, and visions, that present themselves to us, perhaps from a deeper, implicate order, at different times, yet always as archetypal pictures. And we are able to understand these pictures as they appear from eon to eon, through the different levels of our perception and intelligence. We're probably more "intelligent" now than we have ever been. We have more data, more theory, and more processing, that allows us to do better model-making now than ever. We have far more to deal with in terms of knowledge and science. This may be the kind of clue that tells us about the hidden order. Yet in spite of our better intelligence and information, the basic model of the fundamental process remains identical: *as above so below, as within so without.*

What Is Consciousness?

Perhaps the most important piece of evidence we have of the existence of the matrix from which we all appear comes from the activity of mind—consciousness. Consciousness seems to be a process where an environment and an observer of that environment become defined simultaneously. That action, which may not require thought, but which nonetheless seems to require some kind of awareness, causes a split between the subject and object—between the "out there" and the "in here," or between the self and the not-self. Consciousness enables each of us to refer to ourselves as individual entities, separate from the outside world. When we are awake, once having learned to direct the stream of consciousness that bubbles within us, we are inundated with images, sensations, events, and possibilities. In normal waking consciousness we lose touch with the process and we simply take it for granted. In sleep and dreaming, without any significant interruption from outside, our bodies prepare us for direct contact.

It seems that the dream is the place where we learn how to become aware and to separate an "out there" from an "in here." The dream is a laboratory of the self-creation. In this lab an entity becomes defined to itself. It's a self-referencing process, and the self-referencing process appears to be absolutely necessary for any kind of consciousness to occur. Hence we dream to awaken ourselves to the continual birthing experience of life.

The Creation of the Little Self

Some researchers suggest that early humans began to dream in order to survive. The dream induced a kind of paralysis keeping the dreamer immobile. In this way the dreamer would avoid predators. Dream researcher Montague Ullman suggests that we don't dream, necessarily, for individual survival, but that we dream for species survival.[7] Many tribal peoples, in fact, recognize the use of dreams for group survival. They use the dream state, for example, to find food or to escape predators or enemies. So, although we exist as individuals, we continually find ourselves as part of a family, collection, nation, pod, or, in general, part of a larger group of creatures, thus indicating something more than mere individual survival at stake.

Individuation seems to be an important aspect of survival. But why? What is "my self"? Why do I even recognize myself as an individual separate from other individuals? Well, let's look at it this way. If I am a member of a tribe, my concept of self is different than if I am, say, a member of a closed family unit. My behavior, in turn, depends on how I see myself. For example, soldiers fighting in a war view themselves as part of a larger unit; and they behave quite differently toward those outside of their unit, particularly enemies, than they would if they were village people greeting strangers. Thus, how we become aware of the world around us is to a large extent dependent on how we think about our individuality in relation to our environment.

Dreams are vital for the formation of a self, but the concept of the self is ever-changing. The self isn't necessarily just a "skin-box." For example, aboriginal dreaming may involve a concept of the self which is far different from our concept of self. It seems that aboriginal peoples have an awareness of themselves that borders on telepathy. That is, they seem to be aware of situations that we would normally not be aware of, such as being aware that one of their group, at some distance away, is in trouble. So while someone might, say, have to call us on the telephone in order to make us aware of such a situation, aboriginal peoples seem to have a knowing that comes from intuition—flashes of awareness—which they later check when they return to the tribal situation.

In the '70s and '80s, Ullman, Stanley Krippner, and a number of others conducted research on telepathy and dream states.[8] They came to some conclusions, which have been substantiated, that it is possible to have telepathic states of awareness during dreams.[9] In other words, an awakened person and a dreaming person can have a telepathic communication from one to the other. This would indicate that the dream state itself is where this ability developed. For an aboriginal tribe it was vital that they have this telepathic awareness develop, whereas for our culture it seems as if it's not.[10]

Why There's Only One Mind in the Whole Universe

Quantum physics offers many possibilities for explaining the paranormal. Physics, in general, does as well. The question is not so much, "Oh, wow! Gee whiz, why didn't we know this?" The question is more, which possible mechanism is the one we can test to find out what's going on? It's a complex issue, much more complicated than it was when there was nothing in physics to explain it.

To put it simply, or in the most general terms, all of the mechanisms physics has presented are based upon the notion that time and space themselves are not primary, but rather that they are somewhat secondary, and that there is an implicate order in the universe, as David Bohm put it, which is primal to space and time itself. And at the level of the implicate order, the separations of space and time that we take for granted in our everyday worldview don't exist.

So, if there is a process of thinking or communication, or some sort of planning at this primal level below space and time, then when it emerged into space and time it would be simultaneously knowable in a number of different places or times, or both. People who are able to communicate at the level of Unity, or Oneness, or Implicate Order, therefore, could go there and find some form of communication where separation does not exist. Then, when they separate, it would appear as if they had communicated over a vast distance, when actually there was no distance involved at all.

It's another dimension, you might say. It's hard to find the correct words to describe it. Bohm used the example of a fish in a tank, swimming back and forth. In the world that we're in, as we watch this fish swimming back and forth there's nothing unusual going on; it's just one fish swimming back and forth. But if we allow the swimming fish to be the analogy of the primal, implicate-order world that we normally don't see, then the explicate-order world—our ordinary worldview—would be the world we would see if two television cameras were focused on the fish. Let's say that one camera is focused on the fish as it swims right to left, the other as it swims on the adjacent side of the aquarium, so that you could see the fish approaching and then receding. You'd see the head growing and then you'd see a flip, and suddenly the tail would be growing, then diminishing.

Then it would flip, and you would see the head growing again. Now, if the two television cameras were sending information out into space and time to two different receivers, one receiver would be getting the information of head-tail, head-tail, and the other would be getting the information right-left, right-left. When the two receivers compared the data, they would say, "There must be some kind of psychic communication between head-tail and right-left." They wouldn't understand that there was only one object to begin with. They would think that there were two objects, and that somehow they were connected. So the whole notion is that "psychic" or "telepathic" awareness could be a movement into the One, where there is no separation, and then a movement back out into the duality, where there is separation.

Where Does the Dream Come From?

Another way to talk about the implicate order of David Bohm's vision, as I just discussed above, would be to call it the *imaginal realm*. It's a hidden order, the world that we tap into when we go into the dream state. It's the world from which we extract information to use in our physical world. It's akin to Plato's Ideal World. It's akin to the worlds to which shamans go when they perform healings or when they seek information. There is some possibility that under certain meditative states, we could tap into that world and alter what is happening there in such a way that seeming miracles occur.

It is suggested, for example, that Sai Baba of India, whom many consider to be an avatar, is able to enter the imaginal realm, either because of training or inherent ability, and manifest objects, seemingly lifting them from the imaginal realm into this world. It's almost as if he has a window through which he can reach across time and space and pull objects from where they are and bring them into our worldview—like the fish that

I mentioned earlier. Whether Sai Baba's feats are true or not, I do not know. It may just be that he is simply a very good conjurer, which to our Western minds would be the most comfortable explanation.

One might say that all the UFO phenomena going on—the tremendous number of sightings and supposed abductions—is a manifestation of the imaginal realm. Some philosophers, scientists, and visionaries seem to think that maybe the imaginal realm is being tapped collectively, and that what people are getting out of it, either in dreams or altered states of consciousness—or in the abduction scenarios themselves, which are very much like dreams—is an objective experience of that realm, in which there's a certain similarity, based upon some conditioning of the culture as a whole.

There is evidence that over the centuries people are conditioned by their cultures to perceive things from the imaginal which are suggestive of the culture. For example, Irish culture is steeped in lore of leprechauns and fairies. It is no surprise, then, that during the eighteenth and nineteenth century many Irish people reported sightings of leprechauns and fairies.

In a more recent but similar way, American culture is steeped in science fiction. Over the past eighty years or so, books, movies, and television have depicted strange space creatures. From Jules Verne, to *The Day the Earth Stood Still*, to *Star Trek*, the American psyche is steeped in images of aliens. So it's possible that these images originated from the imaginal realm of the authors and filmmakers, then emerged in their consciousness when they had the idea to write a book or make a movie. The images then emerged again in the dreaming brains—or altered-consciousness-state brains—of the people experiencing UFO phenomena. It may be that they're not actually seeing creatures from another space dimension emerging in our world as physical objects, but that they are tapping into the imaginal realm, which is somewhere between "real" and "fantasy," but which has some elements of both.

This is not meant to belittle these experiences or to say that they are merely hallucinations. I am simply suggesting that the brain may work in more of a collective manner than we in the Western world have yet addressed. This idea is certainly a part of the aboriginal culture; it's a part of folklore culture, too. It may be something the Western world should take a closer look at.

Life Is but a Dream

Day to day, we face life as a series of creative moments—ever-changing into something new and yet something familiar at the same time. The incessant bubbling of the implicate order, or the void state into the material world of space and time, alters the "out there" and "in here" worlds of our minds by continually presenting them with new information. Births manifest as thoughts, feelings, intuitions, and sensations. Together they enable us to experience the boundary dividing the inner and outer worlds. When we dream, the process is focused most intently on the inner world; when we are awake, it is focused most intently on the outer world. When we realize that both worlds exist, or come from the deeper more fundamental void—or aleph—we are able to tap creativity and engage in creative lives.

In the next chapter we will examine how to do this—how to make our creations move.

ghimel (ג, 3)

to

lammed (ל, 30)

Ghimel represents movement, the motion of all bayts (matter) containing aleph (spirit). In order for movement to exist, space-time is necessary; so ghimel may be viewed as the primary seed of space-time.

Ghimel transforms into lammed each time we take a step, have a new idea, or set anything into motion. While ghimel represents the urge to move, primal and unconscious, lammed represents an organic whole motion. The slithering of a snake, the flow of a dancer, the ballet-like grace of a wide receiver catching a football, these movements arise when ghimel transforms into lammed. And key to this transformation is feeling. Everything alive feels.

CHAPTER 3

The Wave of Feeling

Life is a wave, which in no two consecutive moments of its existence is composed of the same particles.

John Tyndall

At one point or another, we all have had the experience of being overwhelmed by a feeling. We have also experienced sudden insights, seemingly arising out of nowhere and providing us with flashes of intuition. These inner visions often guide our future actions and hint at what will occur in the time "just around the corner." Most often we are hardly aware of the movement until it just happens, pops into our minds and bodies, and then we feel overwhelmed. It rushes over us, we often say, like a wave—a description that is, I believe, more than a simple metaphor, as I shall explore in this chapter.

In *Mind into Matter*, I explained that the first principle of alchemy is *as above so below, as within so without*. This might be taken to be the mystic's axiom, for it points to the relevance of comparing or making metaphors of our inner life with the objects and movements we see "out there." I also explained how the four basic elements—earth, air, water, and fire—are connected to our sensual experiences.

Aristotle asserted that each of the primary elements was discovered because it possessed two sensual *qualities*—each taken from one of two opposing pairs: hot/cold and moist/dry. Thus, fire appears to our senses as dry and hot relative to its opposite, water, which feels moist and cold; air appears hot and moist relative to its opposite, earth, which appears cold and dry. Hence if one held in one's hand, so to speak, a substance that felt chiefly hot and wet, then one held a substance made essentially of air, vapor, or ether; if it felt cold and dry, it was made mostly of earth. To transform any substance, then, we would need to change one or more of the qualities in the substance. For example, by driving out moisture from a substance the opposite quality, dryness, emerges. The material would then have either or both of the elements of fire and earth whereas when it was wet it had either or both of the elements of air and water.

We all are familiar with these elements and their various combinations. A carbonated drink, for example, contains the elements of air and water. It therefore feels moist or wet, and also cold. Most importantly, our familiarity has to do not with the element possessing properties that we sense, but with the ability of the element to pass on that sensual quality to a physical apparatus such as the skin or tongue. That passage defines what I mean by "transformation." Hence a jalapeño pepper feels hot to our taste buds because the fire element in the pepper passes its heat to our tongues in the form of an acidic chemical reaction. In doing so the pepper becomes colder; it loses its fire. My point being that the sensation we call tasting arises from elements transforming from one thing to another. Life consists of transformation—a movement of the alchemical wave.

Each of us sees and feels the wind, the rain, the sun, and the ground we walk on. We directly experience the four elements of air, water, fire, and earth. Generally speaking, we know that water feels wet and cold, that fire feels hot and dry. We know that the earth generally feels dry and cold. Yet the air blowing against our skin often feels cool and dry. Air appears comparatively warmer than earth and wetter than fire, so it manifests the attributes of wet and warm as in, for example, how the balmy air of the southern climates of the United States feels against our skin.

Life consists of acts of alchemical transformation taking place on a wide range of time scales. These processes occur so often that we commonly accept them without thought or care. When we are uncomfortable with our environment we seek to change the alchemical formulation that leads to our discomfort. We add a log to the fire, turn up the heat or air conditioner, open or close the window, boil or cool the tea we drink, and alter the lighting in our rooms. All of the "out there" world we sense around us continuously arises through alchemical transformations. Hence, it is no wonder that the new alchemy also seeks to describe the transformations involving our inner world of sensation, thought, intuition, and feeling in a similar manner. Imagine as many transformations as you can—"out there" sensations—as I take you into the inner world of your feelings and their transformations. Here we will discover the rules of the inner alchemy—the rules of the alchemical wave of life. But first, to set the stage for our discovery, let me carefully go through the transformations we see occurring in the "out there" world.

THE MAJOR OBJECTIVE
ELEMENTS "OUT THERE"

In brief, there are four major elements composing the "out there" world: fire, earth, water, and air (see figure 3.1). Each element represents an objective limitation of the "out there" world. The limits arise to our senses; they appear to exist independently of the inner world we call our minds. Each element gives rise to two attributes or inner qualities. For example, fire excites our sense of hot and dry. Fire appears to our eyes as light or to our skin as warmth. We taste fire in spicy foods like jalapeño peppers. Thus fire excites the visual, tactile, and taste senses.

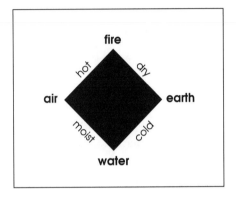

Figure 3.1. The Outer Elements and Their Inner Qualities.

Earth excites our sense of dry and cold. This doesn't necessarily mean that we always feel the earth beneath our feet as cold. (We all know what hot sand feels like!) It just means that the earth element by itself is cold. Of course when we add fire to the earth we have hot sand, or a volcanic eruption. Earth is also, generally, dry. (But, again, we all know what wet sand feels like.) Earth appears to us in the material substances of everyday life. Our bodies are made of carbon, hydrogen, oxygen, sodium, and other earth elements. We literally consume the earth when we eat earth elements. We also excrete earth elements. And we are aware of the earth through touching, tasting, seeing, and smelling.

Note that both earth and fire provide a similar inner experience—that of dryness. What distinguishes earth from fire is the mutability of hot and cold. Given a mysterious substance, we would classify it as fire- or earth-like depending on the degree of cold or heat we feel when we sense the substance. We would say here that fire and earth hold the degree of dry/wet constant (both are dry) and hot/cold variable. (Remember this distinction when we investigate the inner elements of thought and sensation.)

Note also that both water and earth excite the same inner quality of cold. Hence water and earth hold the hot/cold degree constant (both are cold) and the dry/wet degree variable. (Remember this when we look at feeling and sensation.) Continuing along this track we see that water and air hold the wet/dry degree constant (both are wet) and the hot/cold degree variable. (Remember this when we compare feeling and intuition.) And continuing on, we find fire and air are both hot with the degree of wet/dry variable. (Remember this when we compare thought and intuition.)

These four outer elements transform amongst themselves by exchanging their "inner" complementary sensual qualities (hot to cold or dry to moist) on a variable scale. For example, hot runs to warm and from warm to cold. When the exchange is complete, one element is transformed into another. Imagine, for example, holding a balloon filled with water. Now, we will add energy to the water in the balloon by heating the water, carefully, without breaking the balloon. As we experience the change in sensation of cold to hot, it makes sense that we would see the fire content in the material increase as the water heats up and as the water evaporates. When it fills with fire, the balloon expands and rises. The fire increases the movement of the molecules contained within the balloon and soon all of the water is evaporated and changed into air. Thus in the balloon we have a substance that remains just as wet as it was before we added heat to it, but that clearly is no longer water. It has become the substance that possesses or excites the inner qualities of wet and hot, namely air, or, if you wish, water vapor.

It's important to point to the nature of all transformations, namely that they occur in stages where one complementary attribute (for example, wet/dry) remains fixed or constant and the other complementary attribute (in this example, hot/cold) changes. All transformations work in this staged manner. Before a liquid (water) can change to its complementary opposite, fire, it first must become either air or earth and then from this secondary stage it can transform farther into fire. Of course, it is possible to transform an element into its complement or opposite by changing each attribute with one following the other. We could, for example, have further transformed the wet air in the balloon into fire by adding an electrical disturbance and thus ionizing and decomposing the water molecules into hydrogen and oxygen. Later when these elements recombined into water vapor, a powerful fire would be emitted. Such fire was used in the transportation of space vehicles to the Moon and Mars and in the launching of global satellites (where liquid hydrogen and oxygen were burned to give off water and heat energy).

Objective Transformations

In brief, then, we have the following table of transformations:

Changing air to water (while holding dampness constant)
   and its reverse.
Changing fire to earth (while holding dryness constant)
   and its reverse.
Changing water to earth (while holding coldness constant)
   and its reverse.
Changing air to fire (while holding heat constant)
   and its reverse.

The process of changing air to water is illustrated by the condensation that occurs on your windshield on a cold morning following a warm evening. Here the water vapor appearing as the air element changes into liquid upon contact with the cold windshield. During this process the amount of moisture remains the same but the temperature or degree of hot/cold changes.

The process of changing fire to earth (matter) is illustrated by the formation of heavy elements during the death of a star. In a true physical alchemy, lighter elements within a star's interior fuse together, becoming more massive, and sink into its core, producing its radiant energy. As the star radiates throughout its life, its central core gradually turns into iron—the most stable element in the periodic table. Once the star begins to form its iron core, nuclear fusion within that core no longer produces radiant energy. Instead, fusion within the core now absorbs energy producing new elements heavier than iron. At this stage the nuclear stellar fire literally changes into earth in the form of these heavier-than-iron elements. Successively, from the slow and steady bombardment of neutrons, even more massive nuclei, such as gold or lead, form within the core, causing the star to eventually die. In its final death throe, the star expels from its core a gaseous envelope of heavy elements into space and dies, in a last breath, so to speak, becoming a dim white dwarf.

The process of changing water to earth is illustrated by freezing cold water into ice. Here the temperature or degree of hot/cold remains fixed while the degree of dryness/wetness obviously changes from wet to dry.

And the process of changing air to fire is illustrated by heating a gas, which leads to an explosion—as when water vapor expands when more heat is added.

We see many of the above processes occurring in our weather; sometimes all of them taking place within a few moments. The atmosphere is totally governed by the alchemical transformation of water into air (forming clouds) or air into water (forming rain or snow).

The seasons of the year are also associated with the alchemical elements and their transformations. Summer with fire, fall with earth, winter with water, and spring with air. It is no wonder, then, that there are four seasons. Just as hot becomes cold, summer/fire transforms into fall/earth; as the dry earth becomes wet with rain and snow, fall/earth transforms into winter/water; as the cold damp earth warms up, winter/water transforms into the spring/air; and the cycle is completed when the moist air dries and changes into the hot days of summer/fire.

Ain't life grand!

THE MAJOR SUBJECTIVE ELEMENTS "IN HERE"

Just as there are four major elements composing the "out there" world (as seen in figure 3.1), there are also four major elements composing the "in here" world (as seen in figure 3.2). As we saw above, the outer objective elements are experienced in terms of pairs of "in here" sensory qualities. For example, the objective quality of fire is experienced by the subjective qualities of hot and dry. Following along the path of the first principle of new alchemy, *as above so below, as within so without,* here we deal with the four inner elements and their transformations.

It makes sense—in a complementary way—that each of these subjective qualities should be experienced by bookend pairs of "out there" objective attributes just as each of the objective qualities are experienced by pairs of subjective qualities. In effect, we point to the very nature of psychology—the logical measure of the inner psyche as determined by its relationship with the objective qualities of the outside world, just as the logical measure of the outside world is determined by its relationship with the subjective qualities of the inner psyche.

And in the same way that the four outer elements mutate by changing one subjective quality for its complement, our inner elements transform by exchanging their outer complementary experiential objective qualities. In figure 3.2. we see these inner elements (thinking, sensing, feeling, and intuiting) and their outer objective complementary qualities (time/energy and motion/spatial location). Let's look at these in some detail.

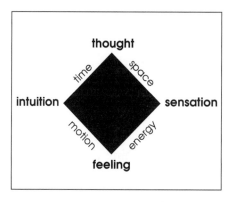

Figure 3.2. The Inner Elements and Their Outer Qualities.

Fire and Thought

Just as fire was experienced as a combination of the sensations of hot and dry, thought projects itself both as processes that appear in our brains and bodies and as objects we experience in the world. Thus thought projects the outer qualities of time and space. Time and space are, therefore, the measure of thought. And any attempt to measure thought certainly involves some form of location in space (as, for example, in our brains or heads) and some recognition of time (as when we remember an event or compare one event with a later or earlier event). Indeed thought is primarily concerned with time and space.

Earth and Sensation

Just as earth was experienced through a combination of the sensations of cold and dry, the inner experience of sensation projects itself both as processes that appear in our bodies as our common senses of the objects we experience in the world and as possessing an energetic quality. For example, some sensations appear to be mild, others strong. Thus sensation arises by projecting the outer qualities of energy and space. And therefore, energy and spatial location are the measure of sensation. We experience sensation in space, indeed it is through sensations that we associate where an object is located, as when we see a star or hear an approaching car. Thus any attempt to measure sensation involves locating something in space. When we locate an object, we do this in space by projecting our sensations "out there" to where we believe the object exists.

Water and Feeling

Just as water was experienced as a combination of the sensations of cold and moist, feeling projects itself as the experience of motion and energy. We tend to feel mildly or strongly about things and events that arise. We also sense an urgency in our feelings, a tendency to move one thing or another as a result of the feeling. Feelings aren't "out there" in space and time, but they project dynamic qualities of movement and energy to things we see "out there." When we see things move or change, we tend to feel. Feelings can directly generate sensations or intuitions, but not thoughts. Thoughts arise from feelings only after we intuit or sense something. Feelings always possess an energetic quality.

As we know, feelings can be mild, strong, or even overwhelming. Filmmakers in particular are aware of this fact and use it to their advantage. As one well known teacher of filmmaking told me, a good movie "makes people feel." When I asked him what, specifically, audiences should feel, he responded, "Anything." Thus feeling arises by projecting the outer qualities of energy and motion. Energy and motion are the measure of feeling. We experience feeling as energy, indeed through our feelings we associate just how strongly we respond to each and every situation we find before us. And thus any attempt to measure feeling involves some form of energetic response as to strength. We also act according to our feelings. Depending on the energy of the feeling, then, we put events in movement accordingly.

Air and Intuition

Just as air was experienced as a combination of the sensations of hot and moist, intuition projects itself both as an outer and inner quality. We tend to order our intuitions through our expectations, so that when an intuition arises we generally sense a feeling of *déjà vu*. Hence intuition projects motion in the world, and a sense of time. Time and motion, then, are the measure of intuition. And any attempt to measure intuition certainly involves some form of temporal awareness, as to when an event is expected. Intuition arises through movement; when we see an object moving we intuit where it will be next. We use our eyes when we intuit. We watch a golfer, for example, and intuit where the ball is likely to be just after the golfer tees off. Our ability to follow the ball depends on that intuition, which in turn depends on our sense of time and movement of the ball.

As Without So Within

Let me summarize the phrase *as above so below, as within so without* by comparing figures 3.1 and 3.2. The positioning of the elements in each figure is deliberate. Fire (the outer element) directly corresponds with thought (the inner element), air with intuition, water with feeling, and sensation with earth.

"Can this be proven scientifically?" you might ask. This is more or less an intuitive picture, although I can offer a brief explanation. Thought, like fire, is associated with rapid change. It cannot be pinned down; it escapes the minute it arises. Sensation requires an object, a material or earth-like substance, to be present to our senses. Feelings, like water, flow over us; they never appear pointed or localized. We sense them much as we sense an ocean wave. Intuition, like air, seems invisible; we don't see it coming, and it appears to have no solidity to it—hence our easy mistrust of our intuitions. So like a cloud in the invisible air, an intuition just pops onto the scene or gradually fills the space of our mind.

Similar plausibility arguments can be offered for each of the outer elements and their correspondences with the inner elements depicted in the same position in each figure. In fact, I will refer to these correspondences as the primary metaphors: fire/thinking, earth/sensing, water/feeling, and air/intuiting.

SUBJECTIVE TRANSFORMATIONS

Now, let's go on and look at the four cycles of subjective transformation in relation to objective transformations.

based on air/water transformations . . .
 Changing an intuition to a feeling (while motion remains constant) and its reverse

based on fire/earth transformations . . .
 Changing a thought to a sensation (while position remains constant) and its reverse

based on water/earth transformations . . .
 Changing a feeling to a sensation (while energy remains constant) and its reverse

based on air/fire transformations . . .
 Changing an intuition to a thought (while time remains constant) and its reverse

Changing an Intuition to a Feeling

Intuition involves awareness of time and movement. It enables us to sense a movement in the future. It always involves movement and momentum, but not necessarily energy. Although movement and energy are related very closely, energy has no direction associated with it, while movement always has a direction. For example, in a football game a quarterback intuits which of his receivers will be free on the next play. He sees the play in his mind; he runs a time sequence through his head; he knows in which direction he will throw the ball, and when. He does all of this without any thought at all, even though he is aware of timing. When he begins the play, he transforms his time-motion intuition into an energy-motion feeling by throwing the ball to the receiver when he feels the pass will be completed. In this way he changes time awareness into energy awareness. He must do this for any action to occur. The ball has weight and inertia; his arm movement requires him to throw the ball with a certain amount of force, hence energy. And all of this is done without any thought at all. (Note the constancy of movement here and the change from time to energy.)

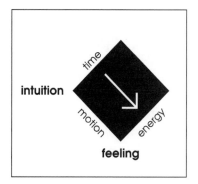 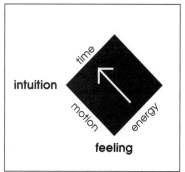

Figure 3.3. The Transformation of Intuition into Feeling and Its Reverse.

The same thing occurs with jazz musicians as they energize their intuitions about playing their music. They turn these intuitions into physical form by exerting energy when they play their instruments.

Reverse: Changing a Feeling to an Intuition

Feeling involves awareness of motion and energy. It involves energy and is the motivating force or source of power. It enables us to take action without any thought at all. A jazz clarinetist, for example, feels the music as he plays it. He feels energized and alert. When he momentarily breaks from play he intuits how he will play the next lick. When he begins the process, he transforms his energy-motion feeling into a time-motion intuition by changing the energy of playing back into time awareness, thus enabling himself to intuit the next sequence—in fact, the emergence of timed sequences is the key, whether it's in playing music, playing sports, or making business decisions. And all this can be done without any thought at all. (Note the constancy of movement here and the change from energy to time.)

Changing an Intuition to a Thought

As mentioned above, intuition involves awareness of time and movement. For example, a business manager intuits that one of his products will sell well in a particular market. So he writes down his intuition as, say, a sales plan or the sketch of a floor display or a table of projected sales figures. He literally lays out his thought by committing it to paper. Thought, involving awareness of time and space, enables us to form plans of action. Changing an intuition into a thought involves transformation of awareness of movement into awareness of location in space-time. Time awareness is constant. In the above example this means that the manager "sees" his intuition

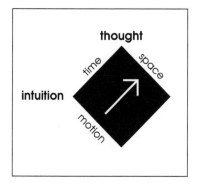 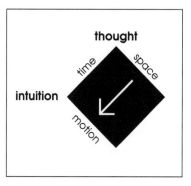

Figure 3.4. The Transformation of Intuition into Thought and Its Reverse.

turned into a well-honed and timed plan of action. Every step in time is accounted for.

Reverse: Changing a Thought to an Intuition

Thought enables us to form plans of action. So as we put a plan (a thought) into action—meaning we allow motion to take place—intuition about the course and direction of the plan continues to arise. Again temporal awareness remains fixed. To see all of this, imagine a dancer who after learning a new routine begins to dance and intuit each new step. While learning the new choreography she uses her intuition and transforms it into thought. After learning the new dance she begins to transform her thoughts into motion using her intuition to get the steps right. As she moves she realizes that her first thoughts were incorrect, and she changes her newly-formed intuition into corrected thoughts, so that her performance improves. Here the transformation continues from thought to intuition back to thought again. Timing remains fixed, for the performance depends on her completing her movements in a specified interval of time dictated by a musical score.

Changing a Thought to a Sensation

As mentioned above, thought involves awareness of time and space and enables us to form plans of action. Thought always involves time and is necessary for a sense of time. Thought always deals with ordering things in time and space. For example, a wine taster thinks about which of his wines will have a chocolaty flavor. When he begins to taste the wine, he transforms his space-time thought into a space-energy sensation by sipping the wine and experiencing it as tasting chocolaty. All of this can be done without any feeling at all. Here the constancy of spatial awareness exists at the palate and tip of the taster's tongue. But to savor the wine he must use energy—the energy involved in acquiring the taste. Literally all of his consciousness is focused in the taste buds. In contrast to the time manager or dancer, the wine taster loses any sense of time during the transformation from his thoughts to his tongue, hence the change in awareness from time to energy.

Reverse: Changing a Sensation to a Thought

Sensation involves awareness of space and energy. It enables us to deal with the objective outside world of our experience.

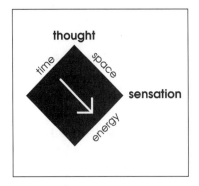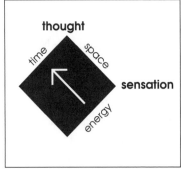

Figure 3.5. The Transformation of Thought into Sensation and Its Reverse.

Indeed it tells us that we are, in fact, having an experience of the outside world. When sensation transforms into thought, awareness of energy shifts to its complement, awareness of time. In the above example, the wine taster, in beginning to taste the wine, thinks about the flavor. He transforms the space-energy sensation at his tongue into a space-time thought by noting that the wine has a chocolaty flavor. Again no feelings arise. Here the spatial awareness, the focus of attention on the tongue and taste buds, remains fixed. However the awareness shifts from the energy of tasting to the time of registering thought.

Changing a Sensation to a Feeling

Sensation always involves energy and awareness of the space around us. Feeling involves our awareness of movement and energy with no regard to the space around us. A business manager, for example, observes a salesperson in action. He listens to the salesperson's words, notices her fragrance, watches her mannerisms and language, and then discerns his feelings. He transforms space-energy sensations into motion-energy feeling. He takes action based on the feeling that this particular

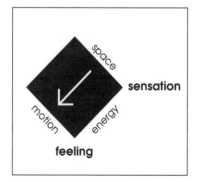
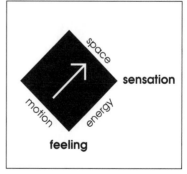

Figure 3.6. The Transformation of Sensation into Feeling and Its Reverse.

salesperson will be good for selling a particular product. In the above example the fixed energy involved in the transformation from the manager's sensations (the salesperson's voice and her fragrance) to his feelings are thoughtless (thought and time awareness are completely unnoticed). The change in awareness moves from space to movement—here the movement of the manager's body and nervous system.

Reverse: Changing a Feeling to a Sensation

Feeling involves awareness of motion and energy. It enables us to take action without any thought at all. In the above example, after the manager assesses his feelings he continues to observe the sales person. He now attempts to apply the reverse transformation by checking his feelings with his next observation to reaffirm his previous sensations. The same energy persists and again he is not thinking, just comparing his feelings with his sensations. The process continues throughout his evaluation.

Summary: Subjective Transformations

As we have seen, the above four transformations and their reverses all involve a change in subjective awareness. They also involve changes of the four objective qualities: spatial, temporal, energy, and motion awareness. Most often these subjective transformations involve completing a cycle of four phases. For example, we could transform a body sensation to a feeling (phase 1) and then the feeling to an intuition (phase 2) and the intuition to a thought (phase 3) that finally completes with the thought returning once again to the body sensation (phase 4) that started the cycle.

There are always two possible pathways through any cycle, clockwise and counterclockwise, as I'll explain in more detail below. However, no subjective cycle can be completed without each of the above four qualities changing while their complementary qualities remain fixed. In this next section we will look at how these qualities behave as we compare constants and variables during a cycle.

Constants and Variables: The Two Cycles of Life

Life passes according to our awareness. And our awareness depends critically upon how we observe each passing moment of our lives. We become aware by putting our attention on things that appear to exist in time and space with the qualities of energy and motion. Depending on how we do this, we experience the changes in our lives through our sensations, intuitions, feelings, and thoughts. The movement of life may at times seem chaotic, but it is not. It moves like a gigantic wave and we are caught atop it. If we try to direct the wave, we will find ourselves in constant battle with it. If we learn merely to survive in the wave's wake, we become victims of it. But we do have another option: we can grasp the rules of the wave's movement and learn to surf it skillfully.

Normally we live our lives utilizing all of the above transformations. Indeed, it would be hard to imagine just what life would be about without using all of them. In fact, as you may have surmised by now, we rarely just use two or three of the phases as we transform life's qualities. Most often we use complete cycles of transformation.

As I mentioned, there are only two cyclic paths possible (see figure 3.2 above), a clockwise and a counterclockwise turning. Surfing life's wave, like surfing an ocean wave, requires your continual awareness. Just as a surfer knows how to pay attention (that is, in which direction to turn his cycle) in order to stay with the wave and avoid wipeout, we can learn to use these two counter-circling pathways as we make life's choices.

How we use complete cycles chiefly depends on understanding which quality remains fixed while its complement undergoes change during any phase of transformation.

In figures 3.7 and 3.8, I have indicated the objective qualities of life: time, space, energy, and movement. Opposite pairs are connected by double-headed arrows indicating transformation of the subjective inner worlds of our minds and feelings. There are only two variables: changing time into energy and its reverse (as seen in figure 3.7); and changing movement into spatial location and its reverse (as seen in figure 3.8). Let me explain this in some detail.

During a time-to-energy transformation, two different things can change within us, depending on what we choose to hold constant—what we wish to see not change. On the left side of figure 3.7, we deal with the inner world of our feelings and intuitions. We do not deal with the question "How can we

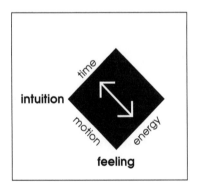
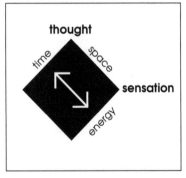

Figure 3.7. The Transformation of Time into Energy and Its Reverse. The transformation of time into energy can produce either a feeling or a bodily sensation depending on what does not change during this transformation. An intuition changes into a feeling with no change in consciousness of motion and with no spatial awareness, while a thought changes into a sensation without any change in bodily position or location, but no awareness of movement.

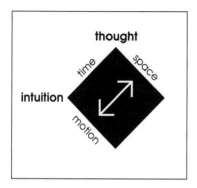
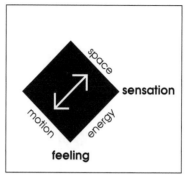

Figure 3.8. The Transformation of Motion into Space and Its Reverse. The transformation of movement into spatial stillness can produce either a thought or a body sensation, depending on what does not change during this transformation. An intuition changes into a thought instantaneously with no awareness of energy, while a feeling changes into a sensation over an indeterminate and unaware period of time. The energy involved in the transformation remains constant. That is why our feelings change so easily into emotions, when energy remains fixed, which in turn produce the body sensations of joy or sadness, pleasure or pain.

change?" We have no idea where we are at all; we exist in a state of constant movement, the rhythm of our breath alters, the pace of our walk varies, etc. We are deep within ourselves and shifting from time-to-energy awareness and back again. Actually we can see this transformation exhibited in any activity where the state of movement remains unchanged—and by that I mean a consistent pattern of motion, as for example, when we walk at a steady pace. Even as we write a letter this transformation comes into play. The chief part of it remains in the rhythm-to-syncopation-to-rhythm transformation.

But look how easy it is to change our awareness from holding movement constant to holding our spatial location constant (as shown on the right of figure 3.7). Now we have given up any idea of how we are moving. For example, we may be changing our breathing pattern or altering our walking pace. When we do this, intuition no longer transforms into feeling and back again. Instead we are now aware of our body sensations and are using our thoughts—thought transforms into sensation and back again. Here our attention moves from thoughts to our body awareness and back. The same variable occurs—energy-to-time transformation—but the effect on our awareness is quite different.

For example, thinking and tasting involve holding constant our spatial location of the sensation. Here the locus of our concentration remains at the surface of our tongues. We could use the same transformation when playing billiards or golf. Nearly any sport where we find ourselves focusing on the way the body performs involves energy-to-time transformation while holding spatial awareness constant. (You might even be moving while you are focused on where you are, but your movement will not be determined or under your control while you are focused on spatial location. All of this arises from the principle of complementarity.)

As we shift our mind from holding spatial location fixed to maintain a constant state of motion we will automatically be changing the subjective transformation of our life experience. This is an important secret of magic, for as we change what we hold fixed, we also change ourselves in the world and change the world with which we relate. Thus holding spatial awareness constant, we transform thoughts into sensations and back again. Holding movement constant we transform intuitions into feelings and back again.

A similar situation arises with holding time or energy fixed (see figure 3.8). During a motion to spatial location transformation, two different things can change within us depending on whether we choose to hold time or energy constant. We deal with the inner world of transforming our thoughts and intuitions (see the left side of figure 3.8). Here we have no awareness of energy or intensity. Instead we remain fixed on time awareness; we find ourselves literally watching the clock. We are shifting from movement to spatial awareness and possibly back again. We experience this when playing chess or any game where we need to be aware of the time.

But change our awareness from holding time constant to holding our energy fixed (see the right side of figure 3.8) and we involve transformation of feelings and body sensations. When we do this, intuition no longer transforms into thought and back again. Instead, feeling transforms into sensation and back again. Here our attention moves without thought or time awareness from feeling to our body awareness. The same variable occurs—motion-to-space transformation—but the effect on our awareness is quite different.

Police officers, psychologists, business managers, teachers—people who work with people—are aware of this transformation. In these professions we are required to observe those we work with—suspects, patients, employees, students—and make judgments based on our observations. We might appear quite calm and cool and make these judgments without exerting much energy or effort. Often there is not time to think about the situation at hand, but we must observe, have a feeling, and use our senses carefully.

THE TWO CYCLES: AN EXAMPLE

Now that we have seen how each phase of a cycle operates, I thought it would be useful to see how this all works by looking at an example. Perhaps you will see how, by making an appropriate choice, you can actually change the world and your presence in it, as well as learn something new that you may not have perceived before.

Consider a cycle that begins and ends with a thought. The cycle can proceed by circling either as *(a)* thought-sensation-feeling-intuition-thought or as *(b)* thought-intuition-feeling-sensation-thought (see figure 3.2).

Your experience will be quite different depending on which choice you make—that is, which way you choose to complete the cycle. For example, following along path *(a)*: You have some thoughts about a person you have just met. You put your attention on his manner of speaking, his body movement, odor or fragrance, and possibly the touch of his hand, as you may or may not touch the person. These sensations lead you to a feeling about the person. Perhaps his bad smell or poor posture gives rise to feelings of mistrust. Perhaps he is tall and handsome and you feel aroused by his presence and have romantic feelings toward him. These feelings provide you with a sense of repulsion or attraction which lead to intuitions as to how you wish to behave with him in the future. As you meet with the person these intuitions naturally lead to further thoughts about him and the cycle perhaps begins anew.

Let's repeat the same event meeting this person. Only this time following path *(b)*. Your thoughts lead you to an intuition about him, possibly a fantasy about how valuable your being with this person will be or how worthless it would be to ever have him near you again. These intuitions lead you to feelings of arousal or distrust. These feelings lead you to sense his presence with greater care or to possibly blind yourself to sensations, ignoring what you smell or what you hear in his voice. These sensations, or blocking of sensations, lead to more thoughts about him, with you accepting or brushing him off.

As you can see, you could have different impressions of the person with different feelings and second thoughts depending on how you complete the cycle. A bad-smelling person could be a valuable asset to you provided you follow your thoughts with your intuitions instead of your senses. On the other hand, with your sensations following your thoughts, you may find the person appealing because he's so attractive. If you had let your intuition follow your thoughts you may have found him completely untrustworthy and then after establishing your feelings see him in a different light.

It may be useful for you to think of other examples in your own life. You can begin the cycle anywhere you like, as long as you complete it. Assuming, for example, you begin with thought, try following the reverse pathway and see if you end up with the same thoughts you started with.

In chapter 4 we will see how these rules of transformation apply to our memories—recent memories as well as those that are quite ancient and even, possibly, in our genetic code.

dallet (ד, 4)
to
mem (מ, 40)

Dallet represents resistance or response to movement. Dallet appears as the common inertia of materials and plays a vital role in the universe. It is the force of resistance in the universe.

Dallet transforms into mem as primal resistance turns into the waters of memory. Without the ability to change resistance into a record, life could not store information, DNA could not arise, and we would have no idea as to who or what we are. Even the question itself would fail to arise.

CHAPTER 4

A Trickster in Our Memory

I have an existential map; it has "you are here" written all over it.

Steven Wright

Our lives are made up of memories. Memories enable us to create rich stories, histories, excuses, and explanations, all of which are put together from our reconstructed life-scenes. Our cells contain memories of our families, parents, grandparents, and even of our environment. They contain the genetic material of our ancestors, and of their ancestors who lived before human life even existed. We call these memories racial characteristics, genes, DNA, and the like. And we believe we can understand ourselves better if we can understand our memories.

To pluck our memories from wherever we imagine them to be stored, we need to rely on some tools. As I described in *Mind into Matter*, we know of four such tools: intuitions, feelings, thoughts, and senses. With this set of tools we bring forth memory to literally shape our existence—to give it form and meaning, to transform the variables mentioned in the previous chapter so that we bring different combinations of feeling, thought, sensation, and intuition into play. But beware. These tools also have a dark—or what I like to call *trickster*—side. For when we use them, we find that they follow rules—the quantum rules of complementarity. The world turns out to be malleable, infinitely changeable. So, not only are we capable of changing the present, but also the past—at least our memories of it.

Indeed, recent studies of memory have shown that recollections, especially over long periods of time but not exclusively so, often change. We would like to believe that our cherished memories of childhood and other periods in our life are faithful renditions of the past. We would equally like to trust that we have recalled an event that occurred only a few days ago. However, several case studies and many experiments show that memories, even when held with confidence, can be quite erroneous.[1] At times we may even insert into our recall of past events scenes that occurred at different times, melding one memory with another. The same holds true for remembering faces or street locations in a city we once visited.

Long recognized by ancient and indigenous peoples around the world as an aspect of our minds, the trickster distorts our factual recall. Yet he—and I refer to the trickster as he for convenience's sake only—plays a vital role in providing meaning in our lives, making appearances to remind us that we might be deceiving ourselves, that our memories can fool us into believing nearly anything, from a false sense of superiority to an equally false sense of inferiority.

So, in this chapter we will explore how our memories affect everything from the way we feel about ourselves to the way we sense the world around us.[2] We will see the trickster in action, and we will come to understand that this magical fellow is our ally, if we can but learn to deal with him correctly.

THE TRICKSTER MEMORY:
AN EVOLUTION FROM PARALLEL WORLDS

It is 80,000 BCE and you are watching the sun set. It's the quiet time of the day, the time for foraging. Up ahead you come to a familiar landmark. But somehow it looks different to you, something has changed. Perhaps it's the failing light on the tall grass. Or worse, perhaps there is a dreaded creature about to pounce. At any rate, you must choose which way to proceed—the lives of your whole family depend on your making the correct choice.

The last time out, you went to the right. Or was it to the left? You aren't sure. Feeling pressured to make a decision, you go left. As you move hurriedly along what appears to be a familiar path, you sense danger. You try to reassure yourself that you are on the correct path. But just as you begin to relax, the great beast pounces. A sharp pain is all you remember as everything goes black. The scene is over. You are dead.

Hold it. Stop the action. Let's run that by again.

You're at the tall grass. But this time you go right. As you move cautiously along the path, a path that you cannot remember, you have a tingling feeling. It's somehow familiar, and yet different, too. Ahead you see what you are searching for. You gather the firewood and return to your family. The scene ends. You have survived.

It seems cut and dried. Either you survived or you didn't. Right? Well, kind of. You both survived and died back there on that prehistoric veldt. You took both paths. Yet you did choose a single path. You had to. But how did you do both? The answer to this seeming paradox, indeed the realization of such a question, is a product of the parallel-universe theory of quantum physics, and, as it turns out, a key to understanding how memory works—and how it sometimes plays tricks on us.

As fantastic as it may sound, the parallel universe theory posits that there exists, as if on a different but parallel layer, another world, a parallel universe, a duplicate copy, slightly different and yet the same as this one. And not just two parallel worlds, but three, four, and even more—no less than an infinite number of them make up a universe of universes. In each of these universes, you, I, and all the others who live, have lived, will live, will have ever lived, are alive.

And just where is this universe? We can imagine it and the one we are in now as layers of a cake. Surprisingly, we enter each layer when we have an experience; indeed, we have been doing so, perhaps unconsciously, ever since time began.

This radical idea plays a role in our everyday lives and, in fact, actually constitutes our everyday lives. Through understanding how parallel universes work, we gain a firmer perspective on why we experience both suffering and pleasure—how they both arise naturally out of fundamental acts of consciousness, acts that indeed "create" the universe in which we all live. These fundamental acts separate our little pieces of consciousness from the mainstream, drops from the ocean of the ever-present infinite universe of all possible parallel universes. These acts, these senses of "knowing" something, are at the root of all suffering and pleasure. In each of these acts is born the greatest illusion of all, the illusion of "I." This ever-present "I-ness," this constant desire to turn I-ness into our "highness," is the only magic show in town.

Layer Cake Universes

The key to understanding the trickster memory comes largely from understanding how parallel universes arise and how they produce temporal awareness. Time awareness appears through acts of consciousness. It emerges as we become, in a sense, barricaded, so that it seems to us that each of our experiences occurs in a single universal layer. This is much like what a horse experiences when side-blinders are put near its eyes to keep it from being distracted by traffic on a busy street. The effect of it would be as if that experience—the act of consciousness—"pops" the quantum wave of consciousness in a sudden and apparently discontinuous manner in a single universe.[3]

Encompassing all layers of the multi-verse brings to light the holographic Mind of God that makes experience what it is in any one layer. Just as a horse becomes overwhelmed by a busy road when its blinders are removed, so would you if you saw that your experience was simultaneously occurring in an infinite number of universal layers where each layer contained a parallel you! Each layer includes patterns. In any one layer, these patterns look much like a track of bubbles in a high energy physics experiment, or a trail of clouds left by a high flying jet. When these layers of bubbles are superposed on each other, as if each layer were a transparent sheet, an overall pattern appears. This pattern is the universal hologram—the Mind of God. From this vantage point, the complete spatial location, or flow momentum of objects, is observable.

Time appears in a single layer as thought. When seen encompassing all of the layers, time appears as the soul's mind. Time is not a true observable like the momentum of a particle or its spatial location. We can't freeze time, so in a sense time can't be counted as an observable like spatial location. We observe memory sequences when we observe time. Hence there is no time; there are only memory sequences. Or in other words, what we call time is actually a memory sequence. These sequences are recordable in arbitrary ways, and they can be replayed. Thus what we call the past is only a matter of record. There is no such thing as *the* past; there are only memory sequences that are somewhat related to each other. The overall pattern—the soul memory—can be reflected in the individual memory on each layer. The overall pattern, however, and the individual pattern in a single layer, are complementary to each other.[4]

If we look at and count all the memory sequences predicted by quantum mechanics, we find that some sequences occur more often than others. For example, suppose sequence 1 consists of a roughly equal number of heads and tails observed after tossing a coin ten times. That means sequence 1 contains any one of the following sequences: 1a) 5 heads + 5 tails; 1b) 6 heads + 4 tails; or 1c): 4 heads + 6 tails. Suppose sequence 2 consists of a distribution of sequences: 2a) 8 heads + 2 tails; or 2b) 2 heads + 8 tails. Sequences 2a and 2b added together would not occur as often as sequences 1 containing roughly equal numbers of heads and tails.[5]

Could the simple numerical fact that sequences 1 occur more often than sequences 2 have any bearing on the mind? If we assume that the mind exists in all the parallel universes, then all sequences are remembered. The numerical superiority of sequences 1 over sequences 2 means that there are more universes with 1 than with 2—which means more memory sequences with 1 than with 2. If 1 and 2 were occurring in your own mind, you would tend to remember 1 more often than 2. It would appear as a stronger or dominant association in coin tossing. You would then expect that when another sequence of ten tosses takes place, sequences 1 would appear again. In this sense, all factual data are simply a matter of vote, with the majority ruling. However, in spite of its lack of occurrence, or your lack of expecting it to occur again, sequences 2 still exist.

In courtroom scenes, for example, the truth is not known. It is agreed on by jury vote. In a similar sense, when considering several possible memory sequences, your own internal jury decides your past experiences. Legal facts are never presumed; the lengthy processes of jurisprudence lead to them. This ultimately means a polling of the jurists. The paralleling sequences, the ones that appear the most common in human experience, are the ones we notice the most, because these sequences are relatively unchanging. In other words, there are far more sequences suggesting pattern 1 than pattern 2, because there are far more ways to generate roughly equal numbers of heads and tails in a sequence of coin tosses than sequences with a preponderance of one side over the other.

Brainwashing may occur through "voting" in this manner. The brainwashed individual is subjected to a powerful group or individual. His votes are tallied along with the votes of the others. And the majority wins, however that majority is decided.

We could say that there is consciousness in every possible memory sequence—in every possible universe layer. If there are a number of such parallel consciousnesses, so to speak— meaning a number of resonating or kindred spirits, good vibrations, etc.— the mere fact of the sequences being nearly the same in overall effect would lead to a form arising between them, much like an overlap of wispy images produces a thick cloud. This cloud of memory sequences tends to produce a collective memory—one that each individual believes is "the truth."

The collective mind enables individuals to see the world as unchanging, either generating habitual responses to changes or leaving things as they are. What is ahead, then, appears the same as what has already passed. Of course, there are many examples of this. Consider the plight of German Jews during the rise of the Nazis. Many Jews simply refused to believe that anything was changing even though their world was dangerously crumbling around them. When confronted with the prospect of something terrifying happening to us, it is not hard to understand that we would go into this sort of disbelief and denial.

But how and why does our mind trick us?

THE BRAIN HOLOGRAM MAKES
THE TRICKSTER APPEAR

One of the most remarkable inventions made possible by the laser is the hologram. A hologram can be made only because of the coherence properties of light waves, and these coherences are the result of the photon statistics, the ability of two or more photons to enter into the same state. The more photons there are in a given state, the greater the coherence of the light wave.

Our brains and bodies may also operate holographically. Experimental work described by neurosurgeon Karl Pribram indicates that the processes occurring in the brain that we label as internal, such as feeling or hunger, are no different from those processes that register as our senses of the outside world. As Pribram puts it, "Clinical neurological experience tells us that the localizing of a perceptual image is not a simple process. The paradoxical phenomenon of a phantom limb after amputation, for example, makes it unlikely that our experience of receptor stimulation 'resides' where we are apt to localize it."[6]

So, even though it appears that we feel with our fingers and our toes, the evidence is overwhelming that the locations of those feelings are not actually taking place there. In a similar manner we see light that impinges on our retinas and hear sounds that disturb our eardrums, and yet we place the source of those sounds out in space and back in time to their appropriate space-time locations. We do not localize starlight at our retinas, but thousands of light-years away. We do not localize the music of a concert pianist at the basilar membrane of the cochlea, but at the keyboard of the concert piano. We project experience outward from our brains and nervous systems. We learned to do this from childhood. Hence sounds and sights appear "out there." But, even though we have not learned to do this with our sense of touch, it is possible to learn to create a sensation in space where no "skin" or sense organ even exists.

Pribram describes some important experimental work of Nobel prize-winning physiologist Georg von Békésy using touch. After describing some preliminary experiments using vibrators to simultaneously stimulate two fingertips, thereby generating the feeling of vibration between the fingers, Békésy wrote:

> Even more dramatic than this experiment is the one in which two vibrators are placed on the thighs, one above each knee. . . . By training, a [subject] . . . can be made to perceive a sensation that moves continuously from one knee to the other. If the [subject] now spreads the knees apart he will again experience at first a jumping of the sen-

sation from one knee to the other. In time, however, the [subject] will become convinced that the vibratory sensation can be localized in the free space between the knees.[7]

Békésy also writes about his experimental studies of how the mind creates external spatial locations of sensations:

I found the location of sensations in free space to be a very important feature of behavior. To study the matter further I wore two hearing aids that were properly damped so that the sounds could be picked up by means of two microphones on the chest and then transmitted to the two ears without change in pressure amplitude. Stereophonic hearing was well established, but a perception of the distance of sound sources was lost. I shall not forget my frustration in trying to cross the street during rush hour traffic while wearing this transmission system. Almost all the cars seemed to jump suddenly into consciousness, and I was unable to put them in order according to their immediacy.[8]

How can we explain the localization phenomena? It could be that the ultimate explanation resides in the fact that the quantum wave vibrational pattern, from which all experiences arise, manifests internally and externally at the same time. The world of experience appears like the world seen in a hologram—made from wave interference patterns. But before we can grasp the significance of this, we need to look at how a hologram is made.

Briefly, it works this way. Suppose a laser creates a lightwave. Lightwaves from lasers have a precise mathematical form, which I shall designate as $[RW]$, which stands for reference wave. The brackets around the RW are to remind us that this wave has two kinds of information: a phase and an amplitude (as shown in figure 4.1). These two qualities can be pictured as a sweeping second hand on a clock face.[9] The amplitude of the wave is indicated by the length of the clock hand, and its phase by the hour the hand points to. If [RW] were to continue on its merry way without striking an object, nothing would be seen, not even the light wave.

Suppose the light wave [RW] were to strike a recording medium such as a hologram. The hologram acts as a recording instrument for light. To record light, the hologram must absorb the light wave's energy. But, the energy depends on the square of the amplitude of the wave, not on its phase. This "square" is obtained mathematically from the [RW] by a funny kind of multiplication: one imagines the wave [RW] to be multiplied by its mirror image wave (signified by [RW]* where the * reminds us that this is a mirror image wave).

One way to think about the mirror-image wave is to imagine that the hologram generates the mirror wave in response to the light wave. Remember I told you about waves

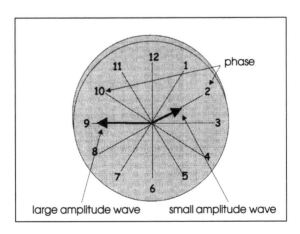

Figure 4.1. Phase and Amplitude. A light wave has both a phase and an amplitude.

having phase. Well, suppose that the wave's phase was at 3:00. The mirror image's phase would then be at 9:00. Then the wave and its mirror reflection multiply together and leave their combined impression in the hologram. When such a multiplication occurs, the phase actually cancels itself out. What happens can be imagined this way: the wave's 3:00 phase is canceled out by the mirror wave's 9:00 phase. The result of the multiplication is the product of the lightwave, $[RW]^*[RW]$, with itself where only the square of the amplitude appears. This is important because the energy representing the recording must never have any phase information. In fact, all recordings are made in this manner.

Now suppose $[RW]$ strikes our eye. Our eye's retina acts just like a recording medium. Again a mirror wave appears and the phase of the light wave is lost. Since what we see is always produced from a recording on our retinas, the images we see are always somewhat incomplete. We don't really perceive $[RW]$, because the eye/brain records $[RW]^*[RW]$. This act of registration is always irreversible, which means we can't get the phase information out once the record has been made. Paradoxically and simultaneously, the retina destroys information in order to record information. Since laser recorded holographic images are also a result of energy deposits made from $[RW]^*[RW]$, such a recording lacking any phase information appears as a uniform and overall darkening of the medium.

This uniform darkening contains no useful information. The key to obtaining a full three-dimensional image does not come from the squared amplitude of the wave, but must somehow come from the phase information of the wave. And to get that, we need to resort to a trick. We need to fool the lightwaves by having them interfere with each other before they strike a recording medium. To do this, we let lightwaves hit an object and be bounced around (as seen in figure 4.2). Lightwaves scattered from an object are affected by the object's form or shape. Thus these scattered waves carry with them piggyback

Figure 4.2. The Hologram. Coherent light waves from a laser [RW] scatter from an object and continue onward, where they and the scattered waves [IW] interfere with each other and are absorbed by a holographic plate.

information about the size and three-dimensional shape of the object. That information is found mainly in the phases of the scattered waves. I call such a scattered wave an *infowave*. This infowave also has a precise mathematical form, which I shall designate as [IW]. Of course not all of the reference wave will scatter from the object, some of it may pass on by. If [IW] and [RW] were to continue on their merry ways without being recorded in some medium such as a photographic emulsion, no hologram could be produced and nothing could be seen.

Now comes the trick. The reference wave [RW] and the infowave [IW] strike the holographic film at the same time. Each wave affects the material of the hologram. So both waves act. The result is that the recorded energy comes from the sum of the two wave amplitudes. In other words, this *superposition* of the two waves, [RW] + [IW], records in the film emulsion with the resulting energy of both waves depositing in the film. But remember, the hologram needs to generate a mirror wave [RW]* + [IW]* in order to make an energy recording.

Then the energy depositing in the film comes from the product of $[RW]^* + [IW]^*$ and $[RW] + [IW]$. If we remember our algebra—$(a + b) \cdot (c + d) = ac + ad + bc + bd$—we see that this will produce four terms.

$$[RW]^*[RW] + [RW]^*[IW] + [IW]^*[RW] + [IW]^*[IW]$$

$$\text{term 1} \qquad \text{term 2} \qquad \text{term 3} \qquad \text{term 4}$$

Now terms 1 and 4, because they are each in reference to themselves, have lost all phase information. Term 1, because it consists of the reference wave interfering with itself, will produce a uniform darkening of the emulsion. Term 4, because it consists of the information wave interfering with itself, will produce a small variation in this darkening, but will also not reproduce any information. But terms 2 and 3 do have information about the object because they each contain both the phase and amplitude information of the $[IW]$ and $[RW]$. Term 2 has $[IW]$ directly, while term 3 has the mirror-reflected infowave, $[IW]^*$. Phase information is not lost here, however, it is hidden because of the reference wave's phase. So now we need to introduce the tricky part: we need to get rid of the reference wave's phase.

The Trick Revealed

Like one of magic's secrets, these four terms are each present and hidden together in the hologram. But they are disguised, and together they form a very complex interference pattern, like the one shown on the hologram in figure 4.3. Like the effort we must exert to see a hidden mechanism prepared by a clever magician, we need to do something to extract any information from the hologram. Hidden in that medium, these four terms contain the important phase relationships

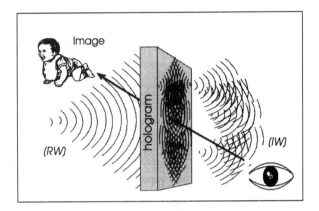

Figure 4.3. The Image Reconstructed. By shining the $[RW]$ through the hologram, the recorded interference pattern generates a virtual image—an illusion of the object in back of the hologram.

that include a record of the whole three-dimensional object. In fact, it contains two such terms.

If we now shine the same $[RW]$ from the laser into the recorded medium of the hologram, it will pass through the hologram, but the pattern in the hologram will block out some of the light and also interfere with the phase of the light. The hologram acts as a filter and the $[RW]$, in attempting to pass through the hologram, has its wave strength and its phase information altered by the presence of the interference pattern in the hologram. Mathematically all we need to do is multiply the $[RW]$ by the terms in the hologram.

Then, the wave that comes through the hologram has the following four terms:

$$[RW] \; [RW]^*[RW] + [RW] \; [RW]^*[IW] +$$
$$\text{term 1} \qquad\qquad \text{term 2}$$

$$[RW] \; [IW]^*[RW] + [RW] \; [IW]^*[IW]$$
$$\text{term 3} \qquad\qquad \text{term 4}$$

Note that the lightwave is on its way after passing through the hologram, looking very much like the interfering light waves that made the hologram in the first place! The hologram diminishes the $[RW]$ by multiplying $[RW]$ by the sum of the four terms. Let's look at each term separately.

Term 1 has three factors: $[RW]$ $[RW]^*$ multiplying $[RW]$. Term 2 also has three factors, with $[RW]$ $[RW]^*$ multiplying $[IW]$. The factors $[RW]$ $[RW]^*$, in effect having no phase information, simply act like a volume control turning down the amplitude. In term 1, the result is a dampened reference wave, but in term 2, the result is the production of a dampened infowave—in other words we've reconstructed the scattered waves from the object and it will look as if an object were really in back of the hologram. In effect, the reference wave has reconstructed the object.

Note especially that term 2 contains the original $[IW]$ diminished in amplitude by the square of the amplitude of the $[RW]$. Hence all of the information produced by the scattered wave is there. If we look in the general direction of the hologram, to the side so as not to blind ourselves from the reference wave direct light, we will see the full three-dimensional object appearing as if it were really there. This is called a virtual image. A virtual image is the kind we see when we look at ourselves in a mirror. The person in the mirror appears to be behind the glass, but we know that isn't so.

What about terms 3 and 4? When $[RW]$ passes through these terms, term 3, made up of three factors, $[RW]$ $[RW]$ $[IW]^*$, appears to generate a mirror infowave, $[IW]^*$ (which I'll get to in a minute). Term 4, having the factors $[IW]^*[IW]$, simply acts like a damper to the $[RW]$.

Since term 3 has two $[RW]$ factors, its reference phase information is not canceled out. If we could cancel it out, term 3 would reproduce a *real* image of that object. A real image is what you see when you watch a motion picture. The projector focuses the light passing through the recorded film image and recreates the image on a screen. Real images can always be focused on a screen while virtual images always appear to be coming from places where they do not exist. To generate the real image, we need to send a mirror reference wave, $[RW]^*$, through the hologram. Then term 3 would look like this: $[RW]^*[RW]\,[IW]^*$, thus producing a dampened $[IW]^*$ wave. Such a wave would appear as an image in front of the screen, right before our eyes, so to speak. Such a real image may be quite important in describing the images that appear in lucid dreams.

The Trickster Memory

As far as human memory is concerned, we can't always know what $[RW]$ will be used. This could account for confused memories. Let me explain. Concerning holograms, when a new light wave, $[NW]$, impinges on the recording medium, it may induce us to see images that weren't really there to begin with. Remember the recording medium acts as a filter, allowing some light to pass through. However, unlike a photographic image that simply reflects a recorded image, it is the interaction of the $[NW]$ with the recorded interference pattern of a hologram that is seen as a three-dimensional image. It is three-dimensional because the $[NW]$ becomes modified by the wave-interference pattern recorded in the emulsion and appears thereby as the original light wave emitted by the object itself (see figure 4.3), or possibly as something completely different.

When a $[NW]$ passes through the medium, the pattern of waves reaching the eye contains the term (term 2): $[NW]$ $[RW]^*[IW]$. If $[NW]$ happens to be the original $[RW]$, this term becomes $[RW]\,[RW]^*[IW]$, the $[RW]^*$ multiplying $[RW]$ wipes out the phase reference information and leaves $[IW]$ unadulterated. Thus when the eye sees this term, it is fooled into thinking that it sees $[IW]$ itself, the information wave that was originally coming from the object. Furthermore, it is fooled into thinking that there is a real object "out there" in back of the recorded medium. This is why this image is a virtual image.

If all sensation is recorded in this manner in the brain cortex, then all sensation will be the reconstruction of objects in space and time from apparent or virtual images of those objects recorded in the cortex. All that we sense as "out there" is projected from our "witness" of the recorded virtual images. This would explain von Békésy's results and, because our minds are reconstructing images, offer as a scientific hypothesis the basis for the age-old Buddhist-Hindu wisdom that "all is maya" (illusion).

We don't sense what we sense; we sense what we remember we sense. And now repeat this phrase replacing "sense" with "smell," "taste," "hear," "see" (and even perhaps "think"). The period of time between the actual event and the movement of the event into the recording cortex is sufficiently small to give us the further temporal illusion that what we sense occurs at the instant the event occurs.

Real Images and Virtual Reality

Earlier I mentioned that when a [NW] was shined through the recording medium, two images were possibly generated, a virtual image and a real one. I then explained how the virtual image appears to be coming from the original space behind the hologram, because the [NW] passing through the hologram is "screened" by the holographic pattern in such a manner that it looks like the light waves coming from the original object.

These light waves can also induce additional information. If a mirror reference wave shines through, it will come to a focus in space, forming a real image of the object. When seen, this image will appear to be floating in space. The reason that

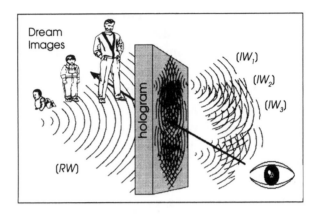

Figure 4.4. Dreams and Memories Are Made of This. By shining the $[RW]$ through the hologram, the recorded interference pattern generates all of the virtual images recorded previously. A similar process in the brain may account for dream images.

this is a real image and not a virtual one is that the light waves actually come from the real image when they are seen. On the other hand, light waves appear to come from a virtual image but actually do not.

In usual applications of holography little attention is paid to the real image because the image is three-dimensional and needs special care in order to be seen. Placing a screen at the focal space of the image only picks up that part of the image that is intercepted by the flat surface, a slice of the image. The virtual image appears three-dimensional but is actually an illusion of three-dimensionality produced by the two-dimensional hologram. The virtual light waves appear to be diverging from a real object in back of the hologram but are actually being formed by the flat hologram. The real light waves, on the other hand, are being focused by the hologram, and the focal points are the points of the image in space in front of the hologram.

Of what use are the real and virtual images in the brain hologram? I suggest that these real and virtual images can be seen when we are asleep. The real images constitute a lucid-type dream while the virtual images make up an ordinary dream. To see how these dreams arise, we need to consider what happens when different objects are encountered at different times in our lives. The brain is again pictured as a recording medium. The $[IW]$s corresponding to the waves of light coming from the different object are denoted as $[IW_1]$, $[IW_2]$, and so on. Each of these waves contains information about an object in question as seen at a specific time, perhaps years ago. These could be bits of computer data, optical pixel information, bits corresponding to sensations, etc.

Suppose that the cortex contains the recorded information obtained from the interference patterns of these objects with a single reference wave. This record was made from the interference pattern produced by the $[NW]$ interfering—adding together—with the $[IW]$s from past events.

If we now look at a series of records recorded in real-time sequence 1, 2, 3, 4, etc.,

$$[RW] + [IW_1] + [IW_2] + [IW_3] + [IW_4] + \ldots$$

they will, upon being recorded, generate the mirror waves

$$[RW]^* + [IW_1]^* + [IW_2]^* + [IW_3]^* + [IW_4]^* + \ldots$$

producing the total memory record

$$\underset{\text{ref term}}{[RW]^*[RW]} + \underset{\text{term 1}}{[RW]^*[IW_1]} + \underset{\text{term 2}}{[RW]^*[IW_2]} +$$

$$\underset{\text{term 3}}{[RW]^*[IW_3]} + \underset{\text{term 4}}{[RW]^*[IW_4]} + \ldots$$

When the $[RW]$ is transmitted through once again, it picks up these terms, yielding the original $[IW]$s themselves.

The result is that when the $[RW]$ is shined through the medium we witness this:

$$[RW][RW]^*([IW_1] + [IW_2] + [IW_3] + [IW_4] + \ldots)$$

with the other terms forming a background of "noise." Since they are added together, these waves form a wave superposition with a resulting interference pattern. This would account for normal dreams.

In the same manner, when we see objects "out there," we not only see them but we replay all the previous information connected to them through past information recordings. The result of this is a replay of the virtual image, an appearance of the image in the outside world. In order to generate this image in the awake mind, the $[RW]$ must come from the outside world. This could be a simple light wave reaching the eye or a sound wave hitting the eardrum. Any outside source of sensation will stimulate the record, producing the image. The superposing of this image together with the actual imposition of outside information constitutes the holographic comparison of a memory with the new outside source of information.

In this way, the continuing newness of experience appears redundant to our minds. We don't ever see just what is "out there" as distinct from our own memory record. Such is the physics of boredom and habituation. Everything is new but we always see our records—it all seems like the same old, same old! Our brains work in this manner in order to ensure our survival. We need to make sure that threats are recognized, thus we need our records.

In essence, our brains are like music lovers who insist on carrying tape recorders with them to the concert. When a piece is performed, the recorder is turned on and plays the same tune the orchestra is playing. And not only do we carry mental tape recorders to concerts but we also insist on playing back every tune that even remotely sounds like the concert performance!

When we have a lucid dream, something else takes place. When we manage to reach that altered state of consciousness, a different tune is played back. Again a new wave is generated, only this time it is not an external wave. The new wave is instead the complex-conjugate reference wave, $[NW] = [RW]^*$.

If we happen to replay the right *wave (star wave) instead of the reference wave—we shine $[RW]^*$ instead of $[RW]$ through our brain caps—the terms that produce virtual images are themselves droned out and the real images of the above experiences are replayed instead:

$$[RW]^*[RW] \; ([IW_1]^* + [IW_2]^* + [IW_3]^* + [IW_4]^* + \ldots)$$

Here the lucid dream starts, where we experience the world at the focus of these *waves. In our dream, we will be awake and will experience sensations and feelings brought on by the actual experiences "learned" in the outside world and that produced the information waves in the first place.

Since these infowaves are *waves, they are the mirror images of our experiences in both time and space. Where one term may have occurred before another, in our dreams they will appear in a time-reversed order. This is akin to directly experiencing our id, where, as Freud pointed out, "logical laws of thought do not apply . . . there is nothing corresponding to the idea of time . . . ."[10] We do experience time in our lucid dream, but it is not real time; it is what our previous information waves told us time was.

By selectively changing the $[RW]$, as we do when we simply look out at the objects surrounding us, we experience

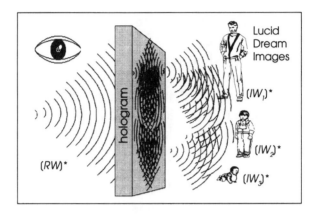

Figure 4.5. Lucid Dreams Are Made of This. By shining the reference star wave $[RW]^*$ through the hologram, the recorded interference pattern generates real images recorded previously. A similar process in the brain may account for lucid dream images.

different sensations and feelings. We have different thoughts and intuitions. Not only does the parallel universes or holographic theory explain memory, it also provides a means to explain how our internal mind world works causing feelings, thoughts, intuitions, and sensations—all we need to feel alive.

In the next chapter, we will see how our memories and observations bring us to a state of agreement and equilibrium allowing life to move from one self to another.

hay (ה, 5)
to
noon (נ, 50)

Hay represents Life, an all-inclusive notion. When there is response (dallet) to motion (ghimel) of material (bayt) moved by spirit (aleph), we have Life.

Hay transforms into noon as the seed-like life form becomes a full-grown living being. For this transformation to occur the seed must break through a shell. This seems to be true throughout the living kingdom. Whether through a nutshell or the vaginal canal, life struggles to be born.

CHAPTER 5

The Curve of Life

Opportunities multiply as they are seized.

Sun Tzu

Although it may not seem so at times, life is a balance between transformation and resistance to transformation. Our bodies exist and feel life because the mind within our bodies urges matter through time. That urge allows life to continue as is, or to change. Cells must come into a kind of balancing act between living and dying. Here we explore one aspect of the nature of this balancing act which shows us that the process is a natural part of life, one that enables life to continue and change, often making new life forms emerge.

Life arises in brief instants punctuated by death. Life, like matter, comes into existence and dies in a punctuated, discontinuous manner, in much the same way that light behaves. Materials emit light in discontinuous bursts. Each burst is called a photon and a photon moves and behaves as if it were made from a continuous wave action, spread out across space and through time like ocean waves rolling onto shore. But when light is observed, it always shows up as it was emitted—punctuated spots—points of light that cause a pixelated series of images to arise on whatever screen the light happens to encounter. Each observation of light is at once the experience of light and the death of the photon itself. Hence the light that we see no longer exists. In a similar manner, the body-self also ceases to exist when it is observed. Let me explain.

From a Buddhist perspective no permanent self, bodily-bound, exists at all. Instead, each self momentarily arises—emitted like a photon—and like a photon traveling through space, carries out the action required for that particular self. With each instant of consciousness generated by one or more of the six senses, that self dies. Each self lives for a tiny instant of perhaps twenty milliseconds and then dies. And as soon as one self dies, another self arises. Thus life is a coherent harmony between these momentary selves.

In this chapter, we will explore one aspect of this quantum view that life is a series of punctuated conscious moments; in the next chapter, we'll explore another aspect of it. We begin here with a lesson in possibilities.

THE BELL-SHAPED CURVE OF LIFE

Life-selves pop up and evaporate like bubbles of foam. Many bubbles appear, making up our living and conscious bodies, and then disappear. Not all at once. If they did, you would be dead! This popping all happens extremely rapidly, so rapidly that we scarcely are aware of it. Much like the frames of a motion picture on a reel passing through a projector create an image and then vanish, our self-awareness of life also passes from instant to instant. We can't count all of the selves, so we need to look at them in a statistical manner. In this way, we can begin to see that these bubbly events form a pattern, or spectrum.

The concept I want to introduce here is called the Gaussian or Maxwellian spectrum distribution. It appears as a bell-shaped, or domed, curve (see figure 5.1). You may be familiar with this curve from your school days, when you received a

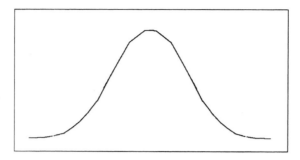

Figure 5.1. The Bell-Shaped Curve of Life.

grade on an exam which had been adjusted in relation to the average class grade; or when your insurance company, to determine your policy rate, used an actuarial table—your position on the curve supposedly indicating how likely you are to live or die, given other factors made equal. Baseball managers use the curve to determine the likeliness of a batter getting a hit in any given circumstance.

Nothing mathematical describes our behavior better than this curve. From the point of view of political expression, the curve also applies. Most of us live cozily nestled on the topmost dome of the curve, near or practically on top of the central point where the average Jane and Joe stands. As far as our behavior is concerned, most of us view ourselves as being among the so-called average or normal people. We include in our view where we stand, what we allow for ourselves in the way of expression and behavior, and what we will or won't tolerate either in ourselves or as a "freedom" given to others.

But the political curve also tells us that there are people among us who deviate from the average. As we move out to either end of the curve—where, frankly, few of us live—we find the extremists, those whose opinions differ dramatically from the norm. For example, if on the right end of the curve we have extremists who want more freedom than we do, and suffer when they sense their freedom being infringed upon, on the left end of the curve we'll find extremists of the opposite ilk—those who feel we have too much freedom and feel pained when others exhibit behavior they cannot tolerate in themselves. These right versus left metaphors often color our talk. We label others with whom we disagree because we're afraid that their opinions will infringe upon our own. So, if we are in the middle of the curve in regard to desire for a certain amount of freedom, we're afraid that the extremists desire for either more or less freedom will affect our experience of freedom—we're afraid we'll be pushed to the right or left of the curve and therefore forced to have more or less freedom than we're comfortable with.

And just as political decision is shaped by this curve, we find in our own behavior a similar "curve of life" shaping our individual choices. We don't always pop on at the exact top of the curve. Each bubble-self can pop on nearly anywhere. But the curve tells us that each self most likely pops on somewhere near the central region, where we find ourselves closely agreeing, or perhaps mildly disagreeing, with our previous pop-on self. This agreement or disagreement constitutes our internal dialogue. It gives us the illusion that an unchanging "I" has agreed to go on as before, or to change course.

This curve influences us because we each are composed of large numbers of selves. There is hardly anything we do that doesn't involve a large number of pop-on events occurring simultaneously or within a small interval of perhaps only a few thousandths of a second. There are about one hundred billion (that is, ten multiplied by itself eleven times, or 10^{11}) neurons in our human nervous system. Each of these neurons activates around ten-thousand feedback loops in connection with other neurons, the outside environment, muscles, and so on. Thus each thought, each brief flash of insight, may be composed of one billion neurons firing, with each one feeding back ten-thousand messages to the environment and to our eyes, fingers, legs, tongues, and other organs.

In his book *The Hedonistic Neuron*, A. Harry Klopf, of the Avionics Laboratory of the Air Force Wright Aeronautical Laboratories at Wright-Patterson Air Force Base in Ohio, showed that we are made of self-indulgent neurons and that these tiny pleasure-seekers are responsible for our memory, learning, and intelligence.[1] Klopf differentiates two conditions of the human nervous system: *homeostasis* and *heterostasis*. Homeostasis refers to a condition where the system attempts to reinforce or maintain a steady or "average" behavior. Such behavior, for example, may be quite consistent with the survival of the person. Heterostasis is defined as the seeking of a goal or maximum condition, a standing above the crowd, so to speak. Our homeostats make us sit at home watching TV, while our heterostats propel us into becoming television stars.

Homeostasis operates through the law of large numbers. Heterostasis doesn't; it abhors the masses—it attempts to move each self off the central bell shape of the curve and onto the wings of extremism. Thus our very thoughts are influenced by this dichotomy. Our "normal" expectations are an outcome of sitting on the dome of the bell, near the average. Our hopes and dreams, on the other hand, are quantum events of heterostatic activity—our desire to use our wings.

Don't Sneer at This!

Every action we take involves this kind of on-off movement. Each time we raise an eyebrow in incredulity, or flare our nostrils in a sneer, a large number of mental events occur. They all fit the bell-shaped curve. Not all of our neurons, muscle fibers, skin patches, and nerve endings want to go along to produce our incredulous sneer at some politician's speech. Some of these bodily components, undoubtedly, want to laugh or even inhibit the actions of the other components composing the sneer. But, as I shall show you next, the homeostatic majority usually wins because it not only outweighs the minority, it also can enforce its average behavior in more and different ways than can our heterostatic behavior modification.[2]

In a society of sneerers, your sneer is expected. You have learned well how to sneer. You have watched your peers sneer. You have learned just how to hold your head, to flare your nostrils, and to condescend. The society of sneerers could conceivably encompass a whole country—perhaps France or England![3] In such a country perhaps sneering becomes an accepted, expected norm, and if we lived in that country perhaps our normal expression would be "sneerful." Thus our faces become the face of a nation. Not only that, but our way of speaking also may be shaped by our faces, our expressions literally shaping the very way we utter a word.

Speech patterns, too, are shaped by the bell curve. Japanese people are known for their inability to pronounce the letter *r*. Japanese children raised in an English-speaking country, however, have no difficulty with *r*. Similar patterns of speech can be found in other language comparisons. German and French peoples have difficulty with the English *th* sound. Likewise, we who speak English fluently may find it difficult to pronounce the French and German *r*.

People may be the same, but their environments shape the life curve and change their acceptable speech patterns. The great desire for normality—that squeeze toward the middle—is reinforced as each person learns the acquired characteristic. As it is with nations, so it goes with neurons. It is not that a sneering nation is compelled to sneer by genetic engineers who have mechanically contrived to produce the sneer. Instead, we have a national alteration of probabilities for each neuron, so that an American neuron is more likely to produce a muscular contortion resulting in a different kind of sneer than the sneer produced by a French neuron.

A Flip of a Coin

The curve of life is dynamic. With each alteration in the probabilities there is a slight shift in the average, much as a batting average shifts slightly every time a baseball player stands in the batter's box, particularly early in the season. Consider again a simple example of coin-flipping. Let's compare the curves representing 16 flips and 32 flips. In figure 5.2, we see two bell-shaped curves representing the probability of seeing heads with a particular number of coin flips. Here we note that the peak in the distribution—corresponding to the average number of heads we would find after completing the flips—shifts from an average of 8 heads out of 16, to an average of 16 heads out of 32, as one might expect.

By altering the number of flips, we are able to shift the curve. So as the number of flips increases, the curve actually broadens and crunches down to take into account that the area of the curve—representing the total probability of one—remains the same.[4] In figure 5.3, with 32 flips we are looking at the comparison of a "loaded" coin flip (roughly 94% probability of heads, 6% tails) with a normal 50/50 coin, where the probability of heads is 50%. The average or expected result with the loaded coin is now 30 out of 32, instead of 16 out of 32.

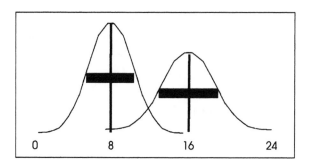

Figure 5.2. The Normal Crosses We Bear.

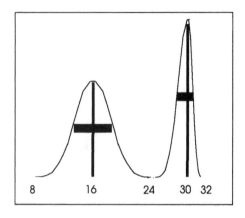

Figure 5.3. The Shift of Normalcy.

Loading a coin to ensure a result is much like acquiring a characteristic that enables us to change our behavior. An acquired characteristic alters the probability by changing neuronal firing patterns. In chapter 3, I explained how we can change our behavior in accordance with the laws of the new alchemy. Here I want to explain why it is that habits are slow to catch on and slow to lose. It's all due to the life curve's mathematical properties, often called the *law of large numbers*.

In figure 5.3, we see how the curve changes as the odds for flipping a coin and getting heads increases. In terms of human behavior, this amounts to an acquisition of a characteristic. Although we are only looking at 32 events, it's enough to make the point. The left-hand, 32-flips curve is centered or normalized on 16 events. This is the situation with, for example, a fair coin (as seen in figure 5.2). The vertical bar marks the norm, and the curve, centered at 16, shows the probability in terms of the number of "successful" events.

The horizontal crossbar marks a length of two *standard deviations*, which in this case is roughly from 13 to 19 and, therefore, 6 "successes" wide.[5] Within this crossbar will lie roughly 2/3rds of the results of 32 coin-toss games. Translating this to human behavior, within this area of the curve we would find so-called normal behavior. We would be tolerant, therefore, of those people whose behavioral patterns remained within this area under the curve. In other words, we tolerate people who fit the norm within a standard deviation of the average. Hence, the cross bar marks our zone of tolerance.

There is about a 2-out-of-3 chance that 32 coin tosses will result in 13 to 19 heads. Moving outside of the "cross of normality" only occurs 1/3rd of the time, and most of that is "gobbled up" by only 1 standard deviation on either side of the cross. Thus the chance you will have from 8 to 12 heads is about 1 out of 6, and about 1 out of 6 that you will see 20 to 24 heads. 6 or 26 heads occur less than 2% of the time, and 28 or 4 heads virtually never occur, with a probability less than 1%.[6]

Now suppose that you are looking at 32 neural events that compose the tiniest flicker of a sneer on the edge of your nostril. With a 50/50 probability distribution, no one could tell the difference, by examining your nose, between your sneer and your smile. Suppose it takes at least 26 successes (that is, in this example, like flipping 26 heads) to make a sneer. Sixteen successes just put your nose under stress! If you couldn't alter the probability of a single neuron "creating" the sneer profile, you would be doomed to sneerlessness.

Indeed, in such a situation your sneerlessness is your homeostasis. Rarely, perhaps in 1 or 2 out of 100 trials, you would successfully don the nostril flair of a true sneer. Perhaps you were watching yourself in a mirror when this rare occurrence took place. You were conscious of your sneer. You even cheered for your sneer. At that moment consciousness entered the game and altered the crap tables of eternity. A small event, no less significant than the grandest, the probability of a single happening, a single neuronal firing, was instantly "collapsed."

The odds of your being able to sneer now have been changed to perhaps 60/40. Suppose after practice and discipline it now occurs, for example, with a 94% probability, or roughly 30 times out of 32.

Your awareness and your intent was all that was needed to shift the average. It provided a feedback for heterostasis to occur. You have learned something. Indeed, your neuron has been trained to sneer. Now the game is suddenly shifted and the tolerance for error has been narrowed. There is still a cross of normality, only this time the normal behavior is marked at roughly 30 successes (as shown on the right side of figure 5.3). The horizontal bar still stretches across 2 standard deviations, but this time it is shorter. It is only about 2½ successes wide. With greater success, little tolerance for error is permitted. Now any number from 29 to 31 successes results in a clearly marked sneer. And this occurs about 2/3rds of the time.

Thus, with an increase in the probability of the event, clearly we would expect more successful events to occur. That explains why 29 to 31 successes are now normal, and less than 28 or an exact 32 hardly ever occurs.[7] But why is the tolerance of error cut down so much? If the probability for a single success were increased to 1, so that every toss produced a success, then it would be impossible to have a failure. There would be no room for it, hence no tolerance for error. The curve would appear as a single vertical bar erected at 32 events. Similarly, if the probability for success were cut down to 0, we would find a vertical bar at 0 events. As the probability for a single success increases from 0 to unity, that vertical bar sweeps across the graph from 0 to 32, and the horizontal crossbar grows in length from a width of 0 events to roughly a full 6 events at 16 successes. From 16 to 32, the bar diminishes to 0 length once again. It seems that nature and statistics give a wide berth to pure chance, but tolerate little error once something is found to be a success or a failure. Much of the theory of evolution, as it describes the success of a species to adapt or not to an environmental change, comes about through this simple mathematical fact.[8]

In this way, life starts off in the tabula rasa, or clean-slate, condition, with all possibilities open to it. In the middle of it all, with success a 50/50 crap game, the tolerance for improvement or failure is greatest. As life goes on, the individual life form learns to adapt—to succeed or fail. The same holds for us. But the price we pay for succeeding or failing is that now there is an expectation put upon us. *Failure breeds failure, while success breeds success.* Although not absolutely guaranteed, it is harder to fail once you have succeeded than it is to succeed in the first place! And, by the way, "hard" simply means the probability is small.

A SMALL LIFE EXPERIMENT

What shifts the curve? The answer turns out to be observation. How does observation change probability? What observes what? To answer the first question, I would like you to try a small experiment. You will need another person for this.

With your partner present, take a coin and flip it so that it spins in the air. Catch the coin so that neither you nor your partner knows which side of the coin is facing you. Now ask your partner this: "What would I say the probability is that the coin hidden under my hand has heads facing up?" Wait a while for your partner to catch on to this tricky question. Remember, you are not asking about the coin; you are asking about your knowledge about the coin.

In a while, your partner will answer "fifty percent." I'm sure that you agree with this utterance for, since you do not know which side of the coin faces you, you have no idea what to expect. Since the coin is a fair coin, both heads and tails are equally likely. But now, while your partner is watching you, peek at the coin, observing which side actually faces you. Repeat the question: "What would I say the probability is that the coin hidden under my hand has heads facing up?"

Of course, the situation has changed, for now you know which side faces up. The answer can no longer be "fifty percent." Your partner will probably chuckle knowingly and say something like "one hundred percent." But that isn't quite correct. The correct answer would be, "It's either one hundred percent or nothing."

Your knowledge of the situation has changed the probability instantly. By becoming aware, you have altered the probability.

I'm sure you realize that this was a tricky situation. Only your "mind" was changed by the knowledge, not the coin itself. You were only observing the coin, so changes in you shouldn't count.

But let's carry this one step further. How do you know that the coin is really heads up (if it actually was when you saw it)? You knew because you knew what heads looked like. If you couldn't tell the difference between heads and tails you would need to learn that difference. To acquire this knowledge, your neurons must be involved in a learning game of pattern recognition. By repeated trials, the pattern is reinforced. And it is only through your ability to recognize the pattern that the reinforcement occurs. Failure to do so results in error. To learn the pattern of the difference between heads and tails, you must alter the probabilities of your neuronal firings. Consciousness enters into this—its function is simply probability alteration through pattern recognition.

These alterations of neuronal firing probabilities produce the experience of normality. Normality may indeed be in error, but our thoughts follow the paths of normality. The paths begin with objects that are remote from our nervous system, relatively uncoupled except through remote interactions. The remote interactions constitute the outside world.

And now that we have explored how the bell-shaped curve of life arises, and have briefly seen how we shift our behavior by using our minds, it is time to take the next step in our inquiry.

The question now becomes: Given that we can adapt and change, what enables there to be sufficient diversification present? In other words, how do the various options open to us arise in the first place? Somehow each of our cells contains possibilities of which a few are brought forward as the cell moves from homeostasis to heterostasis. Where are these possibilities to be found? And even if we find where they are stored as memories, why are they even present to begin with since the cell hadn't been using them? And since it only started to use them when it began to adapt, how did it know what to adapt to?

The answer may seem surprising—the cell must sense out the future and shake hands with it across time. This ability to see ahead, to use the facility of intuition (as explained in chapter 3), enables life to seek out adaptable consequences of change. Not only that, but the ability to do so appears to us in our everyday lives as sex. Thus, as we shall see in the next chapter, a child picks its parents before he or she is even conceived.

vav (ו, 6)
to
sammekh (ס, 60)

Vav represents the copulative element, the "male" energy, the primary or fundamental act of fertilization. Vav is an archetype for potentiality and means "and" in Hebrew.

Vav and sammekh are life's cohorts engaged in the game of survival and creation. They are sexual partners. Vav represents the male seed, sperm motility, while sammekh represents the female seed, stationary and nurturing. Vav runs willy-nilly carrying multiple possibilities of which only a few will actually materialize. Sammekh, too, holds a possibility, but she plays a waiting game. She listens to the future. She senses what might be coming and resonates with it.

CHAPTER 6

Sex: Information Flowing Backward from the Future

You got to be careful if you don't know where you're going, because you might not get there.

Yogi Berra

The partnership of sperm and egg, called gametes in biology, appears to be an adaptation of cellular life, an evolution wherein it became useful, in order to produce biological diversity and enhance survival, to have each cell perform their dance in the well-known manner. The idea is that one cell goes running around while the other remains at rest, so to speak. The game is an exchange of DNA, strips of information. The new cell resulting from this union of sperm and egg appears to have a better chance to survive than either of its parents. It has the opportunity to acquire characteristics and adapt to a new environment that neither parent cell had, because it combines information from both. Simple, yes, but there is an interesting piece of the puzzle missing here.

Changes in environment offer resistance to life. And life either dies or responds, adapts, and thrives. But how? How can the children of life possess characteristics that neither parent had, characteristics that exactly balance the changes in their new environment? Life enables progeny to possess a matrix of possibilities—even possibilities that served no useful purpose for its parents. Suddenly the environment changes and one of the brood finds itself surviving while its siblings are dying. This law seems universal. It applies whether we are talking about the AIDS virus, tuberculosis bacteria, migrating whales, or the family living down the street.

But how did the survivor acquire the characteristic that enabled it to survive? Was it simply born with it? Evolution theory suggests that biological diversity through random processes, enhanced through sexual contact, always produces progeny with random changes—mutations, so to speak—which usually serve no purpose. That is, unless an environmental catastrophe occurs that by sheer chance enables that mutant to live while its siblings die. But, since neither of its parents had the characteristic to begin with, what produced in the progeny the spectrum of diversification that contained exactly the right characteristic to fit the new environment?

Evolution theory does not explain this spectrum. It simply assumes that from random selection, wherein parents choose each other to acquire just the right missing characteristic they don't find in themselves, offspring will arise successfully able to adapt to oncoming environmental change. But how did the parents know? And how did they know that the mix of their gene pools would produce offspring that had the chance to adapt to the new environment? And related to this point, what determines the quantum leaps in the flow of life—the ability to make new life forms emerge? From an alchemical point of view, this process can be discovered in the ancient concept of Adam, whose name means *spirit in blood.* Blood in this case can be taken both metaphorically, as the DNA of the species, or as the red stuff that flows in veins and arteries. Blood nourishes the cells of the body; it also symbolizes the flow of spirit from cell to cell and the flow of spirit from parent to progeny. According to Qabala, the letter-symbols *vav* and *sammekh* refer to male and female sexuality. In general they form the balance between an archetype and its representation in existence. The male seed archetype *vav* (ו, 6) comes into fruition as the female egg *sammekh* (ס, 60).

Here I want to draw attention to a deep connection existing between sexual energy and the relationship of new life forms to past life forms. Although it may seem a remote and strange idea, consider that sexual energy arises from the body's response to time streams calling to it from the future. In a sense, then, we feel sexual because we receive a "phone call" from our progeny yet to be conceived.

These time streams form the basis of the quantum physics of the consciousness-matter relationship, which I'll explain shortly. Certainly we know that sex, as far as nature is concerned, primarily attends future progeny, so this idea may not be all that difficult to grasp. In this chapter, I will show how these time streams work and how they give rise to a sense of flow within each of us and enable the quantum jumps in evolution to occur. We shall see how intuition connects with this time sense.

One interesting development to be explored here is the connection of the momentary selves that arise and vanish through time (as discussed in chapter 5) with the time streams from the future. Here we shall provide a firmer basis for teleology. Indeed the conflict between spirituality and science can be recognized as the clash of two time streams. The spiritual stream, based on the notion of final purpose, represents a flow of information backward from the future to the present; the scientific time stream, based on causation, flows from the past to the future. Their clash is inevitable as we humans attempt to deal with both our need to survive—to keep things as they are, and to evolve—and to make the right choices for our futures.

Time Streams from the Future
and Molecular Evolution

Quantum physics offers a vision of these clashing time streams. It says that both a future event and a present event are required in order that a sequence—a storyline—can arise to connect the two events. Think of the two streams as coming from two waterfalls spaced at opposite ends and emptying into a long channel. As the two counter-streaming flows engage each other, much froth and intermixing occurs, resulting in a form of turbulent chaos. This chaos stirs up all kinds of things in the channel, making new and apparently random events happen. We live in this turbulent mix.

There are many who may scoff at this notion of information arising in the future and affecting the present. But before I get into that, let's consider another objection. Such notions as teleology, even if they do apply in the subatomic world of quantum physics, should play no role in our everyday lives. After all, what does quantum physics, which governs the behavior of atoms, molecules, and subatomic particles, have to do with the evolution of species? The answer, surprisingly, is that molecules, seemingly governed by the rules of quantum physics, also evolve! The evidence for this comes from a book entitled, *The Origins of Life: Evolution as Creation*, in which the author, Hoimar von Ditfurth, offers some interesting hypotheses about evolution and the universe.[1]

Ditfurth sheds light on the controversial debate between creationists and evolutionists. Although he puts down religious fundamentalists and tends to be scientific in his argument, he thinks little of the scientist's materialistic explanation of the source and creation of life. He argues that creation without evolution is nonsense and shows that, conversely, evolution cannot be explained without creation. He thinks that evolution is the Creator's way of governing the world disguised from humankind's limited perspective. It is Ditfurth's explanation of molecular evolution, in particular, that interests me. Just the idea that molecules can evolve sends shivers up my spine. Here is how this works:

There is in existence an enzyme, a molecular fossil, so to speak, responsible for the most basic function of any living cell—intercellular oxidation (the burning of food in the cell to produce energy)—and today the enzyme performs the same function it did when early life began. This enzyme, Cytochrome C, a molecular string composed of 104 amino acids, evolved at the same rate as the species carrying that enzyme, as indicated by the 500-million-year genealogy reconstructed by means of fossil discoveries. Each mutation in that molecular chain can be matched to the appearance of the species that used the enzyme.

By comparing the differences in the Cytochrome C molecular strings obtained from the cells of a human, monkey, dog, rabbit, chicken, frog, tuna, butterfly, mildew and yeast, and wheat, Ditfurth skillfully shows that these differences match fossil discoveries of the species themselves; each species appeared when its Cytochrome C made a change in its molecular structure—in other words, an evolutionary quantum leap.

In considering how the mind came into the world, Ditfurth resolves that "the brain does not produce mind, mind emerges in our consciousness by means of that organ." He concludes that "evolution—supposedly so hostile to religion—has shown us that reality doesn't end where our experience stops . . . evolution compels us to recognize an 'Immanent Transcendence' that immeasurably surpasses our present cognitive horizon."[2]

EVIDENCE OF THE FUTURE INFLUENCING THE PRESENT?

How does a future-generated time stream explain the evolution of the species? First, consider the classical past-causal Darwinian explanation. According to that theory, nature produces copious amounts of genetic material, a gene pool. This gene pool contains, for the most part, the genetic chain molecules that ensure the survival of the species to which that gene pool belongs. Through random genetic mutations produced by random events, certain strains are created that have no chance of surviving in the environment in which they find themselves. For example, during the era in which animals lived in the sea, warm-blooded mutants—animals capable of maintaining their own body temperature, which differed from the ambient seawater—died out. Likewise, albinos did not survive in the strong light conditions found in Africa. Yet these mutations continue to appear from time to time, as purely random events.

It is as if nature continually creates life forms that can survive if the proper environment exists for them, but that die out otherwise. Clearly this cannot be the whole answer. There are far too many possibilities to have to cover all possible future environmental changes. Let me give you an example: the ability of a bacterial strain to survive the onslaught of a future environment created by an antibiotic that hadn't even been invented!

Ditfurth cites the experiments of Nobel Prize–winning microbiologist Joshua Lederberg in which bacteria in petri dishes became resistant to streptomycin. In a series of experiments Lederberg was concerned with adaptation of microorganisms to new antibacterial agents.[3] The question Lederberg faced was were the bacteria pre- or post-adapted. Pre-adaptation meant the resistive bacteria already had the resistance to the antibacterial agent built in genetically. Post-adaptation meant that when confronted with the agent, the bacteria somehow coped. Preadaptation implies that molecules making up a gene had been modified and had mutated. Post-adaptation implies a nonmolecular change in the genes, but perhaps in the chemical environment of the cell when the cell interacts with the agent.

Most adaptation occurs slowly over several generations, suggesting a post-adaptation mechanism. Hence the offspring of a resistive strain may show some tendency to adapt when a hostile environment is presented, but usually most of the offspring do not survive. However, streptomycin seems to induce a single stage of adaptation. In other words, once it is introduced the offspring of the resistant strain continue to resist and survive. This would seem to suggest that somehow some of the ancestral bacteria must have already been genetically modified, that is, pre-adapted, before the introduction of the antibacterial agent, streptomycin. Yet these bacteria existed long before the advent of antibacterial agents.

Lederberg claims that most bacteria are not resistant to antibiotics. If streptomycin was placed in the petri dish nearly all of the bacteria would die, but if any survived, according to the pre-adaptation theory, they would already have been resistant to it. But how could that be? Suppose this strain had somehow existed earlier in time. Then, according to natural selection, this resistant strain should have, in turn, normally died out in the natural environment where streptomycin was not present.

If it did not die out, why would nature hold on to this variant? Clearly in the pre-existent maelstrom of bacterial life, eons before antibacterial agents, no use would have been made of this strain. Hence natural selection should have snuffed it out after countless pre-antibacterial generations. Of course there is the possibility that nature holds on to mutations that do no harm. And, of course, given the number of mutant possibilities that could appear, there would have to be a lot of benign mutants appearing over the long lifeline of these single-celled animals.

In other words, either *(a)* the bacteria knew ahead of time just what characteristic to acquire at just the right time in order to be present when streptomycin appeared (in violation of natural selection); or *(b)* nature somehow produces an infinite number of mutant strains surviving each generation. I somehow doubt either *(a)* or *(b)* separately.

Where does that leave us? Perhaps the answer lies in both *(a)* and *(b)*—albeit a very strange idea.

Quantum Mechanical Evidence of Nonlocality

There is more to the streptomycin story. By separating two identically bred petri dishes of bacteria and putting into one of the dishes the pathogen, streptomycin, thus killing off nearly all the bacteria, Lederberg found, in one tiny corner of the petri dish, survivors resistant to the change. Surprisingly, in the other dish, in the identical corner, he also found bacteria able to resist the pathogen. One might believe that since the two dishes were identically prepared, the pathogen-resistant strain already existed in both dishes, and that nature had already produced the resistant strain just in case she needed it later on when the environment might change. Thus favoring *(a)* above. Lederberg used the technical device known as replica plating that permits one to produce identical cloned colonies of any strain in identical locations on several Petri dishes. In other words, if a particular resistant colony was localized to be at the northwest corner of one dish, clones of that same colony would also appear at the northwest corner of all of the replicant dishes. The key here is that the specifically cloned colonies arise as offspring in the same relative locations on each dish used in the experiment.

There is an alternative explanation, namely, the quantum physics idea of nonlocality. According to this idea, two systems that have had a past interaction will be correlated so that, even though they are no longer in interaction, a measurement performed on one of the systems creates an instantaneous appearance of the attribute measured in the other. Here is what happened: The two dishes were separated after undergoing identical growth patterns. This could not ensure that whatever genetic chain molecule was created in one dish at one site would be exactly reproduced at a like position in the other dish. The two groups of molecules could be, however, quantum physically correlated. Let me explain.

According to quantum physics, molecules cannot possess exact complementary attributes simultaneously. For example, a molecule cannot be in an exact spatial location and simultaneously possess an exact momentum. Quantum-physical correlations exploit this uncertainty. A quantum-physical correlation specifically deals with a measurement performed on one part of a physical system while the other part that had previously been connected to it is left alone. What happens is the measured part (part 1) instantly affects the unmeasured part (part 2) at the moment of measurement, even though there is no longer any connection between the parts. If, for example, the measurer determines the momentum of part 1, the momentum of part 2 is instantly determined. If, on the other hand, the observer measures the position of part 1, the position of part 2 is instantly determined. Thus the similarly located groups of molecules in the two dishes were correlated. When the experimenter changed the conditions in one of the dishes, he produced an instantaneous nonlocal change in the other dish.

Consequently such a correlation would occur in all species previously correlated with each other. It is not that the bacterial strain already contained the resistant molecular arrangement. It was created when the environment "selected" that possibility and turned it into an actuality. Those species evolved that had enriching and parallel-world-splitting interactions. Those that repeated the same processes over and over again did not.

Why Quantum Physics Information?

But this still would not explain how it was that the molecules in the bacteria acquired the required characteristic. Couldn't the required information still exist in the molecules before the invention of streptomycin? Perhaps there wasn't an infinite amount of information existing there, but isn't it possible that natural selection—that is, random events—allowed for the preexistence of this option?

The realization that random selection from already preexistent choices was at best remotely possible while quantum-physical selection based on potential information was pre-eminently conceivable, came to me when I realized that quantum physics information has an infinite potential for fulfillment while classical information can only have a finite potential for achievement. The proof of that comes from today's technology. We are on the edge of a new age of information transfer and generation that makes this clear. The technology called quantum computers will enable us to solve problems that current computer technology is completely unable to solve. Quantum computers are able to do this because quantum information manipulation deals with infinite possibilities while classical information—the kind that we normally deal with in our everyday world—deals with countable actualities.

The elements of quantum information are mind-like, non-energetic entities, wisps and ghosts of potential reality, yet can be shaped by mathematical manipulation. In the vernacular of quantum computers, these manipulatable elements are called *qubits*, and each one is capable of existing in an infinity of potentially possible states, and yet realizable as only one of two actual states—a 0 or a 1. The elements of classical information—bits—are, on the other hand, only capable of realization, either potentially or actually, as 0s or 1s. It stands to reason that, since there are more possibilities imaginable in quantum information manipulation than in classical information manipulation, quantum information enables the realization of more possibilities than are currently already in existence.

So let me return, using quantum-physical reasoning, to the possibilities mentioned above: *(a)* post-adaptation; and *(b)* pre-adaptation. Which one is correct? As I mentioned earlier, perhaps both are. *(a)* works simply because the streptomycin did evoke or, in some sense, *choose* the possibility of survival. Hence without the antibacterial agent this possibility would never have emerged. And *(b)* works because nature did allow the resistant animals to possess the potential for survival from an infinite range of possibilities contained within the quantum domain of infinite possibilities.

This inclusion of infinite possibilities and both *(a)* and *(b)* in the biological structure of the bacterial cell is no different than the fact that a hydrogen atom possesses an infinite range of energy possibilities embedded in its very atomic structure. Any interaction of that atom with any quantum object, such as the scattering of a single photon of light, brings forward this infinite potential. Indeed the scattering of light by atomic hydrogen requires the complete energy level structure of the atom in order to predict the correct scattering cross section observed experimentally.

It's just a matter of counting.

zayn (ז, 7)

to

ayn (ע, 70)

Zayn represents energy in the process of breakdown, a state which enables new possibilities to arise. Zayn is the wave-like field of possibilities grown from the seeds of vav and may also be thought of as the primary principle of indeterminacy.

Zayn and ayn, like the sex partners vav and sammekh that precede them, deal with possibilities. Zayn represents the two flows of possibility: one heading into the future, the other echoing from that future. In ayn these information streams of possibility coalesce and everything that was possible becomes tangibly probable.

CHAPTER 7

The Eye to the Universe

Reality is merely an illusion, albeit a very persistent one.

Albert Einstein

The Hebrew letter-symbol *zayn* deals with flows of unobserved infinite possibilities. No eye perceives them, no ear hears them, nothing senses their presence, and no memory registers them as fact. They remain in the imaginal realm. In the Hebrew letter-symbol *ayn*, we see these information streams of possibility coalesce, and everything that was possible becomes tangibly probable—meaning that each possibility really exists, although each may not be immediately evident. The whirlwind of imaginable realities from the imaginal realm, too uncountable to be fully and totally realized, suddenly manifests into a maelstrom of probable realities. Here we deal with computable, and thereby countable, results of these imaginal flows. Now perception occurs, indeed perhaps many perceptions occur, and all of these perceptions become countable, if we could actually count them, because they have materialized, changed possibilities into probabilities. Mind, guided by the curve of the life force described in chapter 5, has changed into matter. The sheer number of materialized events, often in the billions of billions per second, renders them as statistical entities, subject to many, many influences, mainly the influences they receive from each other.

Ayn, in Hebrew, means *eye* and the two letter-symbols, *zayn* and *ayn*, with the exception of the first letter, are spelled identically—zayn-yod-noon and ayn-yod-noon—no mere coincidence. Zayn indicates the two unobserved flows (indicated by the first letter of its spelling); ayn shows that an observation has occurred in the double flow (indicated by the first letter of its spelling). This observation transforms infinite unobserved possibilities into impracticably countable observed probabilities.

The eye of ayn takes the possibilities of zayn and connects the dots, so to speak, of the "out there" universe with the "in here" mind. The dreams of zayn form into the realities promised by ayn. Hence with ayn a story forms with real, tangible possibilities from the imaginal realm of zayn.

You can think of the eye of ayn as a witness to this story. The creation of the story follows quantum physics rules— observe, disturb, and simultaneously create something from nothing but possibility. When closed or contained within the mind, a time stream flows from the beginning and reflects from the end of the story back to its beginning, like a snake swallowing its tail. A complete history with beginning, middle, and end forms in the mind. When opened or expressed to the world, the internal time stream synchronizes with events happening in the world—or, in other words, the external and internal stories coalesce like two snakes intertwining and still closed on themselves.

This process reoccurs throughout the day and night enabling new memories to form and new information to weave into old memories, like the two snakes relaxing to take a breath of life before re-entwining. In this chapter, we will explore how this occurs as we visit the notion of counter streams of time— one coming from the future and one coming from the past (a subject I began exploring in *Mind into Matter*).

The Mind of God, if anything, is prodigious. Countless imaginings and impracticably countable events continue to appear. Yet we often fail to recognize the novelty of these appearances. We often attempt to turn to the past—"it's just the same old story, the fight for love and glory"—for answers about the present. Survival dictates that we do so. Survival demands that we desire to understand new situations as inevitable consequences of the past, and not as a result of the choices we presently make. We try to make sense of the new, basing it on the old to minimize our risk and responsibility. In other words, we make up a story to fit the sequences of our experiences. We create illusion. The maximum expression of this illusion of risk and responsibility minimization produces a feeling of security. "I failed my examination because the dog ate my term paper." "I was only following orders." "See what you made me do!" And so on.

As we sometimes painfully need to learn, each option carries a risk. We cannot help or stop this process of choosing, risk-taking, and karma buildup resulting from our choices, because these choices must follow quantum rules. They arise as inevitable consequences of the Heisenberg principle of uncertainty and the Bohr principle of complementarity.[1]

DOUBLE YOUR PLEASURE

Changing mind into matter requires feedback from the future, as well as what I call *feedforward* from the past. Feedback from the future appears to the mind as intuition and thought. Feedforward from the past appears as feelings and perceptions of senses.

In order to think and to express our thoughts in words, a script must appear. And it does, amazingly, allowing each of us to complete a sentence or a thought. We can express our thoughts as spoken or written words. The words just seem to pop into existence. Can we will them to appear? While will seems to play some role, it cannot push each word into existence. Somehow words come into mind. I suggest they appear because they are formed from a future's point of view. Similarly, each of us can intuit, form a hunch about what we need to do next, what's coming around the corner of our lives, so to speak. Again, I suggest that the information comes from the yet to be.

Feelings involve energy. Energy is nature's way of remembering, keeping account of the delicate balance of natural processes. Whenever anything in nature occurs, all of the energy involved must be taken into account. No new energy can appear or disappear. In this way, what was present in the past becomes available to the present. Feeling is also nature's way of taking into account the past experiences of the mind. When we see an old friend, one we haven't seen for many years, feelings immediately pop into existence. Often we don't see old friends as they appear now, but as we remember them. How often have you said, when seeing an old friend, "Why it just seems like yesterday . . ."

Sense perceptions are also memories. They are often expressed in terms of likes and dislikes. For example, we all have memories of past smells and tastes. Often they influence how we smell foods, and even influence our taste buds. Whether we like someone or not may be influenced by our sense perceptions—hence the past feedforward mechanism mentioned above.

THE TWO-STEP DANCE OF LIFE AND MEMORY

Through feedback and feedforward, two processes occur: *self-reference* and *re-normalization*. As I discussed in chapter 5, the curve of life continually reshapes itself with each new experience. Here's how it works. Each experience results from the double action of the two flows discussed in chapter 6. There I used the metaphor of time streams. Here I'll use the ancient metaphor adopted from Australian aboriginal people: the two snakes of time. One slithers from the future, the other from the past. Their movement alters the probabilities of events and each alteration pops into reality as a sense of an individual island called "self." Let me label feedforward with the letter F to represent the feedforward from the past to the present, and R to represent the reverse, the feedback from the future to the present.

The basic F and R operations make up a loop in time. Without this loop there would be no "I" sense and no basis for pattern recognition or any memory, feeling, thought, or sensation to even arise. This loop begins with an event, as clearly defined as possible in quantum physics, as *now*, or N. Then a river of possibility flows to a future event, Y (meaning, yet to come), one of several possible future events that have been set up by the N event according to the rules of quantum physics, and then flows backward through or against the time stream, creating a disruptive disturbance. This interaction between the two streams, $N \rightarrow Y$ and $N \leftarrow Y$, gives rise to an observer and an observed—a story and a teller of the story.

A sense of "I" and an apprehension or anticipation of Y forms an intuition. The personal "I" sense, the experience of fear or anxiety, the sense of continuance, and the realization of N as a pattern with respect to the future event Y, make up what we commonly call intuition. Now it is commonly thought that the sense of presence or identity we all feel arises from our memories, that we scan our memories for past events that help us define what to do next. Indeed, we do that, too. But it must be remembered that the "memory" we scan exists now. We aren't literally going back in time for answers to our present problems. I am claiming that we actually look toward the future through this $N \rightarrow Y \rightarrow N$ process, acting as if Y is our memory in the future.

When this double-back flow occurs, a path between N and Y is created so that Y then also occurs. Every event N connects to a past event, P, which N, in a certain sense, caused, and a future event, which from the N perspective is only probable, but from the Y perspective has past. In other words, when an event becomes certain, it is N, and vice versa.

All events that remain undefined through this loop form the great collective unconscious—the Mind of God. These connections define our purpose and our "ourness." Thus suppose there are several possible future events, $Y_1, Y_2 \ldots Y_n$. From the N event perspective, N attempts to connect with all of these future events. Some of the Y events are particularly similar; they differ only in small details and appear overwhelming in number. Without any discernment between the details of the future events—without any attempt to clarify where, what, when, and so on, these events occur—all of the Y events feedback to the "I" event. This results in a strong sense of destiny.

Yet one of the possible Y events will occur. It will become a new N event. Then the next set of Y events will appear. But this time these Y events will differ because they are a realization from a new "I" perspective—the "I"- Y possibilities. A refinement has occurred. And with the realization of yet another Y event, a further refinement will occur.

A Model of Future to Present Refinement

To see this in a model example, I have chosen a simple problem from mathematics. The problem is for an unknown algebraic x to obtain an identity from a possible future form. All x has to go on is that it exists in the future as the number 1 divided by 1 plus itself. Or,

$$x \rightarrow 1/(1 + x)$$
$$\text{past} \rightarrow \text{future}$$

While the above looks like an equation, it really isn't.[2] It means that a substitution needs to be used. The right facing arrow tells us that we need to replace x with a new form, $1/(1 + x)$.

Both the processes of self-reference and re-normalization are going on. In attempting to define itself, x (the unknown appearing on the left-hand side of the arrow) "looks at itself" in a kind of mathematical mirror. Actually, we are doing the looking. We see x on the right-hand side of the arrow in a new form, as 1 divided by itself plus 1. By just guessing any positive value for x, we try to fit x into both expressions.

As x continues by always reaffirming itself in the future, as $1/(1 + x)$, it begins to converge on a value and thus re-normalizes itself.

Thus x, which is a symbol for any number, becomes the same as the number 1 divided by the sum of 1 and x. Now consider the right-hand side of the arrow as the possible future and the left-hand side as the present, or N event. The N event is attempting to define itself by the future. But once this equality is demanded, a restriction is imposed on the variable, x. The x must now *be* something that it wasn't before.

A dynamic process starts off as x tries to fulfill its potential by becoming that which has been imposed from the future. In the next few paragraphs, I'll imagine that x has a mind of its own. The imagined process goes something like this:

What am I? Am I 50? Am I 35? Maybe I'm 100? Let me try x is 50 and see: Does $50 \rightarrow 1/(1 + 50)$? No, of course not. What do I do next? The arrow says that on the right-hand side there is $1/51$, a small number that is equal to .0196. On the left is my starting number, 50, a number I guessed at. It didn't work. But why didn't it work? Let me take the value at the right-hand side, I'll set myself equal to .0196.

Does this work? Does $.0196 \rightarrow 1/(1 + .0196)$? No again. The right side, $1/1.0196$, is equal to .9808. This is bigger than my previous value .0196 and smaller than 50. Perhaps the range of possibility is shrinking. Perhaps x is approaching a real value.

Let me try x as equal to .9806 as the future. Does $.9806 \rightarrow 1/(1 + .9806)$? No again. The right side, $1/1.9806$, is equal to

.5049. This is smaller than .9806 and the range of possible values for x is smaller than before.

Let me try x equal to .5049 on the right-hand side of the arrow. Does .5049 → $1/(1 + .5049)$? No again. The right side, 1/1.5049, equals .6645. This is bigger than .5049.

Let me try x as .6645. Does .6645 → $1/(1 + .6645)$? No again. The right side, 1/1.6645, equals .6008. This is smaller than .6645.

Let me try x as .6008. Does .6008 → $1/(1 + .6008)$? No again. The right side, 1/1.6008, is .6247. This is bigger than .6008.

Let me try x as .6247. Does .6247 → $1/(1 + .6247)$? No again. The right side, 1/1.6247, is .6155. This is smaller than .6247.

Let me try x as .6155. Does .6155 → $1/(1 + .6155)$? No again. The right side, 1/1.6155, is .6190. This is bigger than .6155.

Let me try x as .6190. Does .6190 → $1/(1 + .6190)$?

If you look at x's attempts to gain identity, you will see that while at first it seemed hopeless, there does seem to be a progression taking place. By x trying to identify with a future form of itself, $1/(1 + x)$, x is rapidly converging on a consistent self-referred number. It didn't matter what x was at the start. This process has re-normalized it. If we were to continue this forever, we would eventually find that x could approach but never reach an exact value. At some point the process would stop. We would say that this point was "good enough for all practical purposes." Therefore, for all practical purposes, x is .61803.

Thus self-reference is like this. It is an ongoing process of reappraisal. It stops when it is "good enough." The same is true with our attempts to identify ourselves, to form egos. Each step is an attempt to be that which we cannot be, some form coming from the outside world or some form within ourselves, an ideal image, a hero. The point is that the identity is not in x but in the process by which x attempts to project itself into that which it isn't.

By this process, the future and the present "handshake" across time. Each trial value of x led to a further refinement, with a convergence or re-normalization-identification-realization in consciousness. Since this is a process, it is dynamic. Since it is dynamic back and forth across time, it cannot be "seen" as a physical process. Physical processes occur only along one time direction, from the present to the future.

In the new alchemy, the future decides the present! The past falls under control of the present! Shades of Orwell's *1984*. From the present's point of view, the future is only imaginable as a probability wave. The past is re-membered, re-assembled, re-built, and re-created as a real, past, absolutely fixed-in-the-mind event. Computers, artificial-intelligence devices, and certain robotized individuals known by their stick-to-the-rules philosophies have built-in programs to tell them what to do in novel situations. At least they do something. These "individuals" are intelligent only so far as the past forms the only basis for their present actions.

Human beings are guided by a sense of their own evolved identities in the future, which is why, in general, humans don't seem mechanical. And they're not, in any normal sense of the word.

hhayt (ח, 8)
to
phay (פ, 80)

Hhayt represents the fundamental synthesis of possibilities occurring at the imaginal level, the level where the previous seven letter-symbols also reside. Now, with hhayt, we have the dim beginning of physical existence. Although still a seed, hhayt represents the summing up or storage of the various possibilities represented in zayn.

At the imaginal level, all kinds of possibilities are tried before some of them gel. When the gel forms, the imaginal hhayt turns into the material phay, thus forming the personality of a real being—a face onto the window of life.

CHAPTER 8

From Possibility to Persona and Soul

He who knows that he is Spirit, becomes Spirit, becomes everything; neither gods nor men can prevent him . . . The gods dislike people who get this knowledge . . . The gods love the obscure and hate the obvious.

Brihadaranyaka Upanishad

The Hebrew letter-symbol *hhayt* represents the action of gathering up possibilities, like attempting to brew up the genetic code from daisy seeds in a laboratory flask. The Hebrew letter-symbol *phay* puts this into action, as a gathering of bloomed daisies in the field. With phay, a story unfolds as the two snakes of time (mentioned in chapter 7) bite at the "I"-island of the emerging self, shaping the ego/personality, and making up another episode in each person's life story.

As the snakes nip, two often conflicting plot lines emerge. In one story we ask: How do we as individuals make the best of our lives? In the other story—which is a far more subtle one—we deal with the recognition of ourselves as part of the human picture. In this story, all too difficult for most of us to realize, we see ourselves as part of one mind, rather than as bodies in space and time, distinct and separate from others.

In this subtler story, you, as the individual, play a somewhat secondary role, although you never really lose the individual persona you have created for yourself. As you weave your life story, you find your feelings caught within the web of your own weaving. These feelings embed themselves into what I call your *dream-mask*. Other masked faces show up in your dreams, and in your waking life, and are recognizable as faces of the world stage "out there." Once you are awakened to this process, you are given the opportunity to cleanse, or purify, the face you put "out there" by changing the face you wear "in here," within the collective consciousness of images gathered throughout your life—and possibly even before you were born, but embedded deep within your genetic code.

The process continues throughout life as each time-snake nips at you. The past snake warns you not to upset the interface you have carefully created with the world, while the future snake whispers possibilities into your ear, attempting to awaken your soul awareness by altering that ever-changing, self-absorbed interface.

Here we explore how to bring your persona to face your soul—although admittedly it's never a fully successful endeavor.

BRINGING YOUR PERSONA TO SOUL

Paradoxically, although Buddhists usually profess no belief in the idea of a soul, they recognize the "selfless way," also known as the path of the Boddhisattva. Following this path, each Buddhist vows to save all sentient beings, though they be numberless. Each professes the desire to overcome delusions, though they are inexhaustible, and to follow all of the multiple paths of dharma (good practice), though they are infinite in number.

While this may seem an impossible task, it isn't, so long as we are willing to give up our personas, take off our masks—our egos—as we move through life. Just consider this: Everyone you see "out there" in life or in your dreams is just a mirror of your own unmasked self. Or to put in another way, each is "you," although each wears a different mask/persona, each deals with his or her own karma, seeks his or her own dharma, vows to do, to live, and to play out the role assigned to him or her by the cosmic screen actors' guild.

Taking off your mask, means facing your soul—that face you had before you were born. It means putting the faceless soul on the map of your face, so to speak, right there in the middle of your well-honed personality.

And how do you do this? The solution to this question comes from quantum physics. The world is not as it seems and you are not as you may think you are. Quantum physics enables us to realize that the world is filled with constant change. It shows us that our observations bring the world into existence and as such provide us opportunity to change both it and ourselves. You may try to become immune to the continual changes in life by retreating into illusion—making a better mask for yourself that hides you from others. You may turn your face outward with happy smiles while you remain facing inward, wondering how you will survive the latest onslaught. As you develop a "self-full" personality—a "phayce" onto the world—you tend to forget your original face.

True enough, each one of us needs to deal with local survival issues. We hope for the best, that our soul will take care of the global problems while we "mind our own business." But we feel the world changing and we sense a responsibility. We call this conscience. The conflict between our conscience and our individual needs for survival provides interesting movie plots, and though sometimes it becomes confusing because of our built-in desire for objective or "out there" stimulation, we muddle through, hoping for the best.

Think of this chapter, then, as a guide book—a means to make our personal stories take on greater meaning and happiness in spite of the world we live in, and the events, no matter how tragic, taking place therein. Our first step is to shift our perceptions.

Earlier I discussed the observer effect, which, according to quantum physics, says that there is no reality until that reality is perceived. This profound insight tells us that we alter every object in the world simply by paying attention to it. In this alteration, both the object of our attention and the mind of the observer change. Because we usually don't pay attention to ourselves in the perception process, our immediate experience usually will not appear to show that our actions of perception changed anything. However, if we construct a careful history of our perceptions, they often show us that our way of perceiving indeed changes the course of our personal histories. In the quantum-mechanics world in which we live, we, as observers, ultimately and fundamentally affect the universe whenever we observe it or anything in it.

Thus the world is really not as it seems. It certainly seems to be "out there" independent of us, independent of the choices we might make. Yet quantum physics destroys that idea. What is "out there" depends on what we choose to look for. Although our common sense tells us otherwise, the world isn't made of objects. Instead, the world's objects are linked to our minds in surprising and often mysterious ways. The link is made apparent through the effect our observations play in the world. So, to account for everything we see and do, all that humans observe, we must take into account the act of observation and the role played by the observer's choices.

Mere observation is enough to alter the history of anything or anyone, even a whole country. By observing, each observer disturbs whatever objective observable is present and, as a result, disturbs her- or himself in the process. Yet we hardly notice the disruption. Why? Because each observation creates a memory of the world as existing "out there." That memory replays each time we see a familiar object obscuring the role we play when we choose. Hence our ability to affect the world tends to become obscured. By observing, each observer separates into a self and a thing. Often that thing is one's own face, body, or personality/belief structure.

Consequently, by observing, the observer gains knowledge—but also pays a price. The observer becomes more and more alone and isolated from the thing observed. Perhaps this is what is meant by the Bible's story of the apple and the tree of knowledge in the Garden of Eden. The first bite of the apple is sweet, but costly. Our eyes are opened, and we see a world "out there"—we each see ourselves as alone, separated from everyone and everything. We gain knowledge, and the world becomes alien and strangely unfriendly.

LOSING OUR SOUL AWARENESS

Gaining knowledge has been costly from that very first bite. Each chomp, each bit of knowledge gained, results in a brief "Aha!" followed by an immediate "So what." Yet by becoming conscious of the universe, by paying attention to it, we do transform it. Since the universe includes each of us, the boundary between us and it changes whenever we observe anything. Simply put, it varies because we vary. We are invisibly connected to the whole universe, so the alteration not only occurs within us, but outside of us as well.

We call each occurrence of this alteration an I/it split. Each I/it split results in *consciousness*. Consciousness *is* what consciousness *does*. It performs a dual role in the universe. In the world of quantum physics, it is both the awareness of and the creation of experience. The knowing experience becomes the mind, and the thing being known, matter. The distinction between mind and matter depends chiefly on our choices.

By choosing to see the world one way, complementary ways of experiencing become hidden or inaccessible. While these hidden views no longer appear to mind as objective qualities visible in the world as things, and remembered in the mind as memories, they remain part of the unconscious mind-world as possibilities. Upon a change of choice that brings forward the complementary way of experiencing, these previously hidden views become apparent—"out there"—while the previous qualities vanish in the physical world but remain as the contents of memory. A magician uses this trick to fool us into seeing a thing as it was prior to his sleight of hand. When we choose to see the same thing over and over again, time stops for the observer, a consistency develops, and the qualities being observed remain constant (a concept we recall from chapter 3 when we explored constants and variables).

Here is an example. You meet someone you haven't seen in a long time. It becomes clear to you that the person has aged. Perhaps he has a few wrinkles or his hair has turned gray. In your mind, your relationship with the person will begin where it left off many years ago. In your mind, you will not see the person as he is now, with a few wrinkles and gray hair, but as he was then. Indeed many married couples remain in this highly imaginal realm with each other, even though many things about themselves and their relationship have changed over the years.

In this state, the actual physical person in front of you remains hidden from your sight, even though his current physical appearance may be apparent to others. Changing the way you look at him, bringing your view into the present moment by paying attention to how he looks now, immediately stops the memory from surfacing and also cuts off any feelings you might have had about this person. Suddenly you see him anew. You can then shift your perception from old to new, from old feelings to new sensory information, and in doing so begin to have a wholly different appreciation for the person.

Sometimes it is difficult to realize that you always have a choice in everything you do. While this may seem merely a matter of convenience, it really depends on the quantum physics world we live in and the quantum rules that our world must obey (as I discussed in chapter 1). In order to come to the realization that you always have a choice, you need to become aware each time you feel resistance arising within yourself. The feeling of resistance is the awareness of choice arising within you. It is your continual awareness of the material/spiritual complementarity split, and the fact that you are a spiritual being living in a material world. It can also be noted as the being/becoming split or the quantum physics wave/particle split. In general, it's the flag of awareness telling you that you have a choice involving two complementary ways of experiencing anything.

If you choose the self-full way of seeing, then once you have chosen, once you have chosen your path to be one of knowledge-being-particle, the resistance becomes inertia—a mind object that connects to a physical object "out there." When it arises, you experience your self as separate from the object of your awareness. If, on the other hand, you choose the self-less way of seeing then once you have chosen, once you have chosen your path to be one of heart-becoming-wave, the resistance dissolves—a mind object no longer connects to a physical object "out there." When this choice is realized, you experience your intent dissolving, taking no form at all, and you experience your self as one with all objects. In fact, no object appears separate from you. For some of us choosing to experience "self-less-ness," it appears difficult. And it is difficult, because of the inertial properties of all mind objects (as discussed in chapter 4).

A HIGHER POWER

The complimentary-principle-of-choice process is universal. You can think of the universe operating this way as well. When the universe chooses to be, sees itself materially, it becomes aware of a growing resistance called *material inertia*. This inertia is the same resistance we experience when we discover a new idea. The universe can and does make the alternate choice, and when we are spiritually aware we can sense when it does. By making choices, the universe becomes self-aware. As a material-choosing universe, it transforms information into matter, giving rise to physical objects, and transforms matter into information, giving rise to a mental universe that models the physical. Resistance arises in each transformation. This is the order of the transformational process.

As a spiritual-choosing universe, it becomes what is called a *one-verse*. All space-time-matter remains undifferentiated. This is the Mind of God, where no resistance arises and nothing transforms. No information actually passes from one thing to another because nothing is separated from anything. Everything just shines.

But, you might argue, the world seems so disordered, hardly ever shining in the above manner, there always seems to be something missing. This disruption of God's order appears as the quantum-physical uncertainty principle. Thus we become helpless, feel inadequate, and long for the order we are helpless to create in the universe. All we can do is go along with it.

But we are indeed free to choose. Our very helplessness to create a perfect order allows us to create. Our helplessness invites us to surrender and to recognize that perfect order, as we picture it, cannot exist in the material world. So we might say that the uncertainty principle is a two-edged sword. It frees us from the past because nothing can be predetermined. It gives us the freedom to choose how we go about in the universe. But we cannot predict the results of our choices. We can choose, but we cannot know if our choices will be successful. The beauty is that by choosing to see spiritually, we are no longer interested in prediction. We become one with our soul.

tayt (ט, 9)
to
tsadde (צ, 90)

Tayt represents the cell—any focus or center or concentration of energy—that becomes female. It is the womb, a place for birth to begin.

When tayt manifests, turning into tsadde, it becomes the whole universe of matter and mind. Whereas the final outcome of tayt was cosmic resistance, the final outcome of tsadde is yod— the material universe itself.

CHAPTER 9

The Structure of Love in the Universe

In order to create a universe . . . Parama Shiva brings into operation that aspect of his Shakti which manifests itself as the principle of Negation and lets the ideal Universe disappear from his view and allows Himself, as it were, to feel the want of a Universe, but for which feeling there could be . . . no need of a manifested Universe on the part of one who is all-complete as Himself.

Jagadish Chandra Chatterji

When the Hebrew letter-symbol *tayt* (ט, 9) changes into *tsadde* (צ, 90) something truly remarkable occurs. To explain, let me first review the meaning of tayt.

Bayt, hhayt, and tayt have similar spellings. They are bayt-yod-tav, hhayt-yod-tav, and tayt-yod-tav. The yod-tav endings tell us that these letter-symbols play similar roles in their seed-like actions. They all deal with existence (yod, י, 10) and resistance (tav, ת, 400). Yod symbolizes the world we all inhabit. Tav symbolizes not just any old thing that gets in the way of motion, but a cosmic or final resistance—the end letter of the Hebrew aleph-bayt. And, as I mentioned in chapter 4, resistance is vital to life—without it nothing can come into existence. Tav lets us know that resistance remains a fundamental mystery, as mysterious as anything can.

Bayt, hhayt, and tayt play creative roles and deal with the reflective properties of ultimate resistance, without which nothing real could ever come into being. In bayt the action is explosive and relates to the Big Bang and all fundamental actions of creation; in hhayt the action is synthetic and creative in the ability to pool possibilities; in tayt the action is concentric and creative in the sense of forming a fundamental unit, an object of the mind or physical world. Thus bayt explodes new creative possibilities into being, hhayt takes them all into account through synthesis, and tayt brings them back together in a material form.

The seed-like actions of bayt, hhayt, and tayt occur in the imaginal realm, but once we multiply any of them by ten, they become materially present. When tayt manifests as tsadde, it becomes the whole universe of matter and mind. Tsadde is spelled tsadde-dallet-yod, so whereas the final outcome of tayt was cosmic resistance, tav, the final outcome of tsadde is yod—the material universe itself.

Even more is revealed if we spell out the complete word for tsadde, spelling out the final yod (shown here in italics): tsadde–dallet–*yod–vav–dallet*. It just so happens that dallet-vav-dallet-yod (pronounced *dodi*) means "my beloved," according to the Hebrew version of the Song of Songs.[1] Hence it is no accident that we find these characters emerging here when we open the letters as I have indicated.

And another clue reveals itself if we spell out dodi in reverse—yod-dallet-vav-dallet. We see that this reverse spelling is very similar to the spelling of Yahweh—yod-hay-vav-hay—the only difference being that dallet replaces hay. The master of Qabala, Carlo Suarès, tells us that these two schemes have tremendous importance and form a holy apostasy.[2] Dodi represents, through its two dallets, resistances fertilizing each other into existence. Hence "my beloved" is the one who acts in resistance and response to our own resistance and response. But since dodi's letters are the reverse of the letters of Yahweh—dallet-vav-dallet-yod (instead of yod-dallet-vav-dallet) versus yod-hay-vav-hay—

dodi is actually a response to Yahweh. We commonly feel this response as love and compassion. Accordingly, dodi reflects the love and compassion God has for the universe.

YAHWEH AND LOVE

Tsadde, then, in its evolution from tayt—representing a fundamental cell structure—not only deals with all structures in existence, it contains a secret often mentioned in sacred writing: the universe contains, and God created the universe out of, love. This love and its resultant structural beauty show up in the anatomical formation of tsadde. This structure arises from the unfolding of each letter-symbol in the spelling of tsadde. Hence tsadde contains an infinite number of dallets, all appearing in mirror pairs at every level, as we see in figure 9.1. (Not all of the pairs are shown, of course.)

We all seek love and partnership. It is perhaps the ultimate driving force in our lives and in the universe. From this new alchemical vision, love arises from structures, embedded memories, and the two counter-flowing time streams of our lives, described earlier. According to the mirror structure shown in tsadde, love appears to require partnership. The Hebrew word for earth is eretz, spelled aleph-raysh-tsadde. This literally means spirit (aleph) creates the universe (raysh) in structures (tsadde). Hence the earth, too, was created from love. It has love at its core, in spite of the many scientific views that leave love out of the equation.

Learning to see love and to express that love is the purpose of living this life. My point in this book is to show that what's real has love at its heart; the universe is constructed from love, and that love is very much tied to our power of attention and imagination. Quantum physics and Qabala, as expressed in the new alchemy, may appear extraordinarily exotic, and yet if you're ready to accept the viewpoint it offers, you may see the

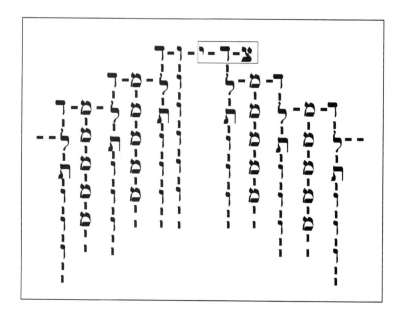

Figure 9.1. The Evolutionary Tree of Tsadde. The three letters in the small rectangle are (reading right to left) tsadde-dallet-yod. Since vav is spelled vav-vav, its opening reveals a rain of vavs. Further expansion of yod on the same line, reading also to the left, gives us vav-dallet, revealing two dallets. Next we open up the spelling of the two dallets (dallet-lammed-tav), illuminating the infinite, complex, and mirrored structures shown. The Hebrew character מ (mem, coming from the spelling of lammed) is spelled mem-mem, hence its similar rain of characters.

nature of your consciousness in a new way. With the help of new alchemy, startling ideas that mystical traditions have embraced for millennia may color your ideas and actions. The idea is to learn to color them in love.

My Love Story, in Brief

I discovered love at an early age. No, I don't mean the love of my family or friends, though certainly that form of love is very important. I'm talking about a larger form of love—one that connects solidly with awe, mystery, and devotion. In my early childhood, I had an interest in magic. I can't remember when I did not have this interest. It propelled me into the study of physics, because the world I perceived around me, even as a child, seemed to have a magical quality. I wondered about a lot of things. And surprisingly, anything I wondered about would eventually pop into my existence, usually not overnight, but eventually it would appear in my life.

I took this quite naturally, but I didn't realize, at the time, how much this was an expression of God's love. The two are connected—love and magic. Just ask any poet or songwriter. Magic seems to be a natural way to inquire into nature. In fact, conjuring, performing magic tricks, wondering how magicians do what they do, led me to study physics, which in turn propelled me into the deeper aspects of physics, then metaphysics, and eventually into mysticism and spirituality.

Are Science and Magic Antithetical?

I found the territory of mysticism and spirituality strangely compelling, and, yes, feelings of mystical delight entered my whole way of being. I hadn't realized that, in a sense, God and I had become lovers. My God showed me love by allowing me to see the deeper magical and abstract world brought forward by the discoveries of theoretical physics. These discoveries were indeed awesome, and I had an overwhelming feeling that they were part of the magical mystery tour called the universe.

I hadn't realized that in becoming a beloved of God, I might seem strange to my fellows. I then realized that I had become "estranged" from the mundane world, and that most scientists who are dedicated to seeking answers to the mysteries of the universe, as I am, are considered bizarre. We make fun of scientists, erect walls around them, placing them as far away as we can from the ordinary world. One would hardly suspect that scientists are motivated by love, but they are. In fact, one of the reasons science came about was to deal with that conflict that arises between the mystical feeling that, I believe, all scientists have, and the need or desire for some kind of explanation, which I attribute to the same need for security we all possess. We want to understand the world in some way. It may not be the same way in different cultures, but we want to have an understanding that enables us to cope with the various probable and improbable things that seem to happen to us from day to day, or over a whole lifetime. Science epitomizes the need to explain nature to ourselves and, as I see it, the need to live in the world with some kind of joy—that joy being what we call the mystical or spiritual experience.

In the mind and heart of every scientist, and I think in all of us, there often arises a conflict between the need to explain and the need to experience the love of the universe. From the new alchemical view, we see this conflict in terms of the complementarity principle discussed earlier. It reflects the basic battle of spirit (aleph) and matter (yod).

I don't think any scientist would ever say that science explains everything. I certainly don't think it does. But neither would any scientist be willing to accept the mystic's view of the world as the last word. There's a continual battle in each of us between spirit and body. In spite of how it may appear, however, love forms the foundation for this war, with time arising on the battleground called the universe.

Love and Uncertainty:
The New Alchemical Foundation of Life

If life teaches us anything, it certainly tells us that we can't know what lies ahead with any certainty. Every life situation arises anew. We turn to the past for answers to the present and hope that these novel situations are inevitable consequences of the choices we made and the chances we took with life. We cannot help or stop the process of risk and karma buildup that results from choices we make. Risk and karma arise as inevitable consequences because the Heisenberg principle of uncertainty and the Bohr principle of complementarity operate in our daily lives. They constantly render the known as unknown, the obvious as hidden.

Suffering always arises because of the seemingly secretive way that God operates. It would appear that God creates problems by allowing people to make choices. Once we see a "problem" one way, we fail to see its opposite side. This failure reinforces it as a problem. The other side of the problem is nothing more than the recognition that if anyone is suffering, you are suffering, we all are suffering. If one blade of grass is crushed, something in you is crushed as well. Recognizing this helps to understand the inevitability of suffering. To relieve the suffering, to free ourselves from any repetitious patterns of self-identification, is usually difficult because it is a humbling and embarrassing feeling. It carries with it the kind of helplessness that we often see in the faces of the very old and the very young.

To relieve such suffering, we need to recognize that each of us has created it. There is hope if we choose to hope. We are the creators of this universe. We shape its raw materials into our fantasies, which we call Reality. We have reached this stage of understanding in the most peculiar way, the Western way of science and industrialization. We have learned to manipulate the physical and have discovered the spiritual.

The next time you find yourself suffering, try this. Become what you hate for a moment. Do this in your thoughts and discuss it with your friends and families. Turning the other cheek or loving your enemy is no act of foolish charity. It is a real solution. By accepting other's foibles as our own, we relieve our suffering.

Quantum Physics and Suffering

Quantum physics and human consciousness are intimately related. The basis for this is the role of the observer in the act of observation. The observer is not passive, but plays a unique role, one that depends on what he or she believes is "out there." (If you look for waves, you find waves; if you look for particles, you find particles.) Thus we humans play a far greater role in our own destinies than we may have originally thought. Indeed, we seem to be ruled by our projections of what is and what isn't. We live by our wits, projecting our abstractions into the physical world.

All of us have two motives in life: to seek joy and avoid pain. Religion arises as the means by which we try to attain this state of bliss. If we take as a tautology that the removal of suffering and the acquiring of joy is religion, then all humans are religious. In this sense, too, the new alchemy is a religion, or will become one, because it appeals to that sense of enlightenment and mystery that we intuitively sense as truth. It offers a solid basis for understanding what is meant by the spiritual or mind element.

The universality of all religions is the recognition of our connection to all living things. This connection is like a chain; whoever pulls it creates a feeling for whoever is attached to it. We cannot help but feel the chains of attachment created by our physical interactions. But the continual repetitious patterns of separate egos act to change, create, and break these connections.

Paramahansa Yogananda states that our lack of bliss—our suffering—is brought on by the process of identification with the transitory body and the restless mind.[3] In the new alchemical view, the two time streams create an endless pursuit of happiness. They continually bounce around changing by the sequences of self-serving choices, which produces a disruption of bliss states. Each sequence of self-referential or biological feedback tends to produce distributions of events that are repeatable and directly sensed as non-threatening and survival enhancing. These operations are inherited from our reptilian and mammalian pasts. They appear to us as powerful urges that at our present state of evolution are no longer needed for either survival or pain avoidance. Indeed, today they act in just the opposite way, threatening us and providing the means of our extinction.

A way to realize joy comes through the insights of the new alchemy, which tells us that matter is not the king of the universe, but rather its love slave. As such, matter rebels and escapes. By realizing that all matter is time-bound, but that the two time streams are bound by neither matter, energy, space, nor time, we have a choice of identification. It is no longer necessary to identify with our fear and our survival. If we identify with our soul, as described in the previous chapter, we all become free. You, in a very real sense, are holding all of us in the palm of your hand. You are the liberator of all sentient life forms.

COMMON SENSE ABOUT OUR UNCOMMON UNIVERSE

I have a lot of faith in my common-sense understanding of the world. I accept the flaws as well as the benefits that come to me as a result of having these common senses. Before I learned this, I would try to get beyond my senses into something which left me solving my original problem, but left me hanging in terms of everything else. I'll give you an example.

You're in a relationship with somebody and something occurs which you find displeasing. You want to correct the situation, so you offer solutions to what you anticipate will be a problem in the future. As a result, you create a conflict, possibly even destroying the relationship. Had you let your common sense guide you, however, you would have realized that all you needed to do was to give your partner a hug. In other words, don't intellectualize everything into a problem when there's really no problem there. Accept that the universe is not a machine, that it can't run entirely by cause-effect apparatuses—human beings are not machines.

This simple insight broadened my understanding so that I am able to understand things commonly, in an ordinary sense, and in a deeper sense as well. We can peel off the layers, go into the deeper levels of what things ultimately mean, and finally reduce our inquiry down to the level of quantum physics and God and Spirit.

Thus we live on a beautiful earth and we experience love—all this without thought. That's the common-sense understanding. We see that from the new alchemy point of view there is a deeper understanding—love in partnership is built into the earth through universal correspondence with Spirit. The people I work with in workshops and those that respond to my writing intuitively work with me in this common, deeper understanding. If I say that I have a firm belief in God, for instance, they know that where I'm coming from is not necessarily just blind belief in a superficial way, but from some deeper experience of belief.

If you follow my thoughts to a logical conclusion, you find that there's only one Soul in the universe. One Consciousness capable of blinking matter into reality and letting it go out of reality. If you are having that experience, then you're having it because you've identified with that single awareness. It's not that you have a mind and Mr. Jones has a mind and Mrs. Smith has a mind, but that you, Jones, and Smith are all of one mind. It may sound nice, may sound spiritual, to say that we're all one mind, but quantum physics actually points to its being true.[4] The blinking on or off is a very important part of it. It indicates that mind, or the One Mind, is very much part of the physical world.

Maya, Illusion, and Multiple Minds?

Let me try to explain the One Mind viewpoint. If the physical world is maya—an illusion—what's real? That is, of course, the question that drives everybody a bit crazy. But reality is not just the physical world; it's the relationship of the mind with the physical world that creates the perception of reality—there is no reality without a perception of reality. If we assume that the world is what it appears to be, even when we're not looking, we evoke an assumption that's fraught with problems.

Quantum physics has been in existence for more than one hundred years, and it consists of a well-defined set of rules which work in a universal way. Yet what it predicts about the world is not how the world appears. It predicts, among other things, strange overlaps of reality, parallel realities, and objects being in two or more places at the same time. Normally, we don't see such a world, but (as discussed in chapter 5) there may be many exceptions to the rule.

In a circular way, the rules of quantum physics say that as long as no one is looking the world should follow the rules of quantum physics. That means that multiple realities should abound. Still, you may wonder, how is it that objects don't appear at two places at the same time, and that the world seems to be a single world. This result, according to our quantum mechanical understanding—often these paradoxes in quantum physics can be resolved through such understanding—comes about whenever an observation occurs. All of the multiplicity in the quantum physics universe pops into a single reality, not multiple realities. When someone looks, one reality appears while the others hide. And that's what mind does. But, what if there are two minds in the world?

There's an ancient philosophical problem that goes something like this: You're standing in a room looking out of the window at a garden. You decide to leave the room and go into the room next door and close the blinds so that the room is completely black. What happened to the garden as a result? The answer, according to quantum physics, is that if you were the only mind that ever was and ever is and ever will be, the garden would turn into multiple gardens the minute you entered into the darkened room.

Most of us have a hard time understanding this, so let me alter the story a little. Suppose there's another person still looking and who still sees the single garden while you're in the dark room seeing nothing. What is that telling you? From a common-sense viewpoint, one person sees light and the other person sees dark. No problem, common sense says, since two people with separate minds exist. But from your darkened, quantum physics viewpoint, both that other person and the garden should inhabit multiple worlds, since you are not looking at either of them. Hence we face a paradox: From your point of view, the world you don't see, including the person in the lighted room, are multiple entities; but from the other's point of view, consciousness has acted and a single garden appears.

Clearly we can't have it both ways. Either there are multiple gardens or not. If not, which common sense dictates, then quantum physics must be incorrect since from your point of view no observation took place. But, if quantum physics is correct, multiple gardens exist. So the person in the lighted room must also be in a multiple state, since you're not looking at him. Yet, if you asked him what state he was in, he'd say that he's perfectly normal and phrenic (as opposed to schizophrenic) and as sane as anybody else. And so we run into a paradox that the world according to the way you see it follows one set of rules, and the world that others tell you about conflicts with your understanding of the world.

This paradox will always arise, so long as minds can be compartmentalized. If a mind can exist independent of yours, then you are allowed to consider its operation as one that must follow quantum rules. Hence that other mind that you don't have any privy to must be schizophrenic. The only way to resolve the paradox is to realize that one mind is capable of seeing both light and dark simultaneously. Once that one mind acts and changes the multiple gardens into a single landscape, it is registered in all minds.

That still leaves a problem unresolved. How can one consciousness exist in what seems to be two parts, and yet still be only one mind? Even though that mind seems to be in two places, it's not. Whatever is conscious in the world cannot be just between your ears, my ears, or the ears of anyone else, but must exist non-locally. It doesn't have any single location. And yet, how can one mind create the illusion of so many minds?

WHAT IS DUALITY?
CAN THE ONE SEPARATE FROM THE ONE?

If you accept that there is only the One Mind, then the experience of the illusion of separateness from the One, of having your own singular existence seemingly separate from the One, must be maya. From this point of view, maya is based on the concept of duality. Without duality, there can't be any separation from the One.

You might answer this paradox by saying that unity is inconceivable. It's unapproachable. It can't even be defined because the mere act of definition would distinguish between one thing and another. That act of definition is, by its nature, duality, or separation.

We have explored the nature of the numbers one and two; one (unity), symbolized by aleph, and two, symbolized by bayt. The symbol of unity or aleph is the great, undivided, power of Spirit. The symbol of bayt, or two, is a house or container symbolized by the action which separates an inside from an outside, or defines a boundary between left and right, or up and down, or any distinction at all.

In a tarot deck, the number two card is often the magician card. It is the act of the magician—bayt, 2—that brings into existence something from something else. The act of bringing into existence something from something else, as if by magic, thus represents duality. The paradox is in recognizing that if we can see a distinction, we follow the magician's trick and fool ourselves. Then there's something within us capable of being fooled by experiencing our sacred unity as profane duality. Maybe that's the way the game of life must be played. The ultimate new alchemical rule of unity is to form duality. Only in this illusion can unity be experienced. We can't begin to conceive of unity without this illusion of duality.

Remember that in tsadde we found everything in mirrored form when we opened the letters. So that for every dallet there was another dallet. Hence to experience the love and beauty of the universe we need to create mirrors. Only in those mirrors can we see unity. Only in the great multiplicity of life can we see the One.

SEEING INTO THE MIRRORS OF MIND

There really is only one Mind, and the thoughts that you're having, while they may seem very personal to you and very self-contained within your own head at the moment, those thoughts are being thought everywhere by everybody at some time in some form. Not necessarily in the same way that you're thinking now, but they're part of a collective consciousness—as Carl Jung would say—or of the One Mind.

I believe that evolution is also part of this One Mind. As life goes on—from the eye blink of several thousand years ago when Buddha and Yeshua walked this planet, to the present moment—a tremendous number of movements have occurred, everything, from the early appearance of Mohammed to the scientific revolution we're experiencing right now. Years ago the scientific renaissance began as a reaction to the mysticism that was clinging to Europe and affecting everything from the politics of kings to the health of people dying of the Black Plague.

The same kinds of conflicts occur today. This means that we're living through an age of mental stress. By that, I mean there is a stress on our natural spiritual inclination to be of One Mind arising from conflicts brought forward by religious secularism and conflicts within the current materialist base of Marxism, Darwinism, and our current scientific materialism. It's as if our minds are being stretched like saran wrap, being pulled across the hands of time. We're caught in the warp and none of us can calmly think our way through it. Instead, we must work our way through the warp, the stress, which reverberates each time we come up with some new insight as to the nature of what is real and what isn't.

So, at times the world may seem to be a very dark place, but the light of the One Mind will always shine through. There's never an end to the shining which comes through the magic present. The mere fact that there is a world at all is so miraculous, so impossible to explain, that we should, in recognition and in faith of that, be continually awestruck and continually joyful, in spite of any lacks we may feel in our daily lives. The fact that we exist in material form is no less miraculous, and it may very well be that the common suffering that we see around us and that we feel within us may be concomitant to, or the result of, the fact that we are spirits living in a material form. We are merely reflections of a single mind in a multiple-reflection looking glass.

Endnotes

Chapter 1
The Island of Feeling We Call the Body

1. In Greek mythology, Narcissus was a handsome youth and many women fell in love with him. But he resisted their advances. Among the lovelorn maidens was the nymph Echo, who had been condemned by a goddess never to speak again except to repeat what was said to her. One day, while in the woods, she heard Narcissus call out. He had become separated from his friends and because of the woods could no longer see them. Upon hearing Narcissus's voice, Echo felt great frustration. Unable to tell Narcissus of her love, she could only repeat what he said. When he shouted, "Is anyone here?" She joyfully answered, "Here, here." But, as he had done with previous lovelorn maidens, when he saw her emerge from the trees, he cruelly refused to accept her. Humiliated, she hid in a cave and wasted away until nothing was left of her but her voice. To punish Narcissus, the avenging goddess Nemesis made him fall hopelessly in love with his own beautiful face as he saw it reflected in a pool. As he gazed in fascination, unable to remove himself from his image, he gradually pined away. At the place where his body had lain grew a beautiful flower, honoring the name and memory of Narcissus.

2. This will be explained further later in the chapter when I discuss Freud.

3. Of course, isotopes exist. But they don't interfere with chemistry.

4. Indeed they did when the early Greeks were theorizing about how atoms looked.

5. John Muir (1838–1914), Scottish-born American naturalist and explorer, who helped establish Yosemite, King's Canyon, and

Sequoia National Parks in the United States, believed that everything was alive with spirit, including animals, trees, rocks, and mountains.

Also see *The World as I See It* (Secaucus, NJ: Carol Publishing Group, 1999), p. 25, where Albert Einstein writes, "The true value of a human being is determined primarily by the measure and the sense in which he has attained to liberation from self."

And see *Across the Frontier* (Woodbridge, CT: Oxbow Press, 1990), p. 141, where Werner Heisenberg writes, "We should not let everything else atrophy in favor of the one organ of rational analysis. . . . It is a matter, rather, of seizing upon reality with all the organs that are given to us, and trusting that this reality will then also reflect the essence of things, the 'one, the good, and the true.' "

6. Although there has been much controversy surrounding him in recent years, in his early writing Da Free John made some very interesting observations concerning the ego. In fact, his early writing, as indicated here, provides remarkable insights which I have found stimulating to my own thinking, particularly in regard to the structure of the ego. So at the risk that some readers may find the man himself disturbing, I hope those same readers may find the ideas I've included here interesting.

Also see the discussion later in this chapter, and endnotes 8 and 9 below.

7. See James Fadiman and Robert Frager, *Personality and Personal Growth* (New York: Harper & Row, 1976). Also see Sigmund Freud, *The Ego and the Id* (New York: W. W. Norton, 1960).

8. Sigmund Freud, *An Outline of Psychoanalysis*, standard edition, vol. 23 (New York: W. W. Norton, 1940, 1949), p. 2. Freud, too, has appeared controversial from time to time as new generations discover him. I don't wish to belabor the point, but often new ideas are accompanied by ideas unpalatable to common tastes and sensibilities.

9. See endnote 6. Also see Da Free John, "On Liberation from Ego and Egoic Society, or, Cooperation + Tolerance = Peace" online at http://adidam.org/gateway/society/beyond_ego/dhome.htm?go= /gateway/society/beyond_ego/ctpfull1.htm, and *The Transcendence of Ego and Egoic Society* (Clearlake, CA: Johannine Daist Communion, 1982).

10. Complementarity exists in both the physical and mental sense. In everyday life you are familiar with complementary colors like red and green. Just as it is not possible to see red and green overlapping together since they wipe each other out producing black or white, we cannot make overlapping complementary observations of our feelings and be able to label those feelings at the same time. This is well-known by counseling psychologists who try to get their patients to talk about their feelings. Once acknowledged, the feeling is known, no longer a mystery, and, therefore, it no longer holds power over the patient.

11. See Paramahansa Yogananda, *Autobiography of a Yogi* (Los Angeles: Self-Realization Fellowship, 1973).

12. See J. Krishnamurti and David Bohm, *The Ending of Time* (San Francisco: HarperSanFrancisco, 1985).

13. See Jane Roberts, *The Unknown Reality*, vol. 1 (Englewood Cliffs, NJ: Prentice-Hall, 1977).

14. Closed surfaces appear either stable or unstable. For example, a closed surface made from four equilateral triangles forms a stable volume called a pyramid. On the other hand, the six square sides of a box form an unstable cube—one that is subject to collapse if conditions or stress rods are not appropriately inserted to maintain the structural integrity. Hence egoic structures like these surfaces may exhibit similar tendencies to self-collapse or remain intact when "outside" forces impact them.

15. At the time of this writing, trapping light, indeed slowing it down to zero speed, has been demonstrated. See Lene Vestergaard Hau, "Frozen Light," *Scientific American* (July 2001).

16. See my book, *Star Wave: Mind, Consciousness, and Quantum Physics* (New York: Macmillan, 1984).

17. I realize that this statement constitutes a scientifically unprovable anthropomorphism.

18. You might want to know why. In quantum physics we discover a rule about states—they exist in complementary pairs. This means that states that do not change in time are said to "possess" precise energy, while states that are specific to particular times do not. All of this relates to the uncertainty principle, which does not allow one to determine either when something occurs or what energy it possesses when it occurs.

19. In chapter 3, I'll simplify this considerably by referring back to the ancient Greek alchemical depiction of earth, air, fire, and water.

20. See endnote 9. And I should point out that my model of the ego presented here was chiefly inspired by Da Free John's remarks that the ego is a self-contraction.

21. See Paramahansa Yogananda, *Autobiography of a Yogi*, 13th ed. (Los Angeles: Self-Realization Fellowship, 1998), p. 47. Also see online http://www.crystalclarity.com/yogananda/chap5/chap5.html.

22. The uncertainty principle explains the impossibility of simultaneously determining an exact location and momentum of any object. It points to the fact that when either momentum or location is known precisely, the other complementary attribute becomes completely indeterminate. Hence once the location of the object is well specified, the momentum takes on a range of possibility that includes near infinite energy.

23. Nothing, except that now the particle is confined to a smaller space. Consequently, any energy changes it suffers will be proportionately larger. Analogously, this results in the contracted ego's undergoing more effort to replicate experience by changes in feeling than before the contraction. In other words, it requires more work and energy to create changes in energy for the boxed particle in the contracted state than in the original state.

24. Just as there are more irrational numbers than rational numbers. Just in case you've forgotten, a rational number is any number produced by division of integers. So, for example, 5/6 is rational. An irrational number is any number than cannot be produced this way, such as the square root of 3 or the famous π, the ratio of the circumference of any circle to its diameter. Consequently, all circles with rational diameters must have irrational circumferences.

CHAPTER 2
From a Dream to Reality

1. Athena sprang full-grown and armored from the forehead of the god Zeus and was his favorite child.

2. Scientists believe that all mammals dream, with the exception of two mammalian species: the spiny anteater, or *echidna*, and whales and dolphins, or *cetacea*. Scientists draw this conclusion because these two species don't exhibit signs of rapid eye movement (REM) when sleeping, REM being indicative of the existence of a dream stage in consciousness.

3. See Jonathan Winson, *Brain and Psyche* (New York: Anchor Press, 1985) and "The Meaning of Dreams," *Scientific American* (November 1990). For other views, see J. Allan Hobson, *The Dreaming Brain: How the Brain Creates both the Sense and the Nonsense of Dreams* (New York: Basic Books, 1988).

4. In *On the Origin of Species by Means of Natural Selection, or the Preservation of Favoured Races in the Struggle for Life* (London: John Murray, 1859), Charles Darwin writes:

> The affinities of all the beings of the same class have sometimes been represented by a great tree. I believe this simile largely speaks the truth. The green and budding twigs may represent existing species; and those produced during each former year may represent the long succession of extinct species . . . The limbs divided into great branches, and these into lesser and lesser branches, were themselves once, when the tree was small, budding twigs; and this connection of the former and present buds by ramifying branches may well represent the classification of all extinct and living species in groups subordinate to groups . . . From the first growth of the tree, many a limb and branch has decayed and dropped off, and these lost branches of various sizes may represent those whole orders, families, and genera which have now no living representatives, and which are known to us only from having been found in a fossil state . . . As buds give rise by growth to fresh buds, and these, if vigorous, branch out and overtop on all a feebler branch, so by generation I believe it has been with the Tree of Life, which fills with its dead and broken branches the crust of the earth, and covers the surface with its ever branching and beautiful ramifications.

You can find Darwin's great work online at http://www.literature.org/authors/darwin-charles/the-origin-of-species.

5. David Bohm's works are discussed in many volumes. For his notion concerning the *implicate order* out of which dreams arise, see David Bohm, *Wholeness and the Implicate Order* (London: Routledge & Kegan Paul, 1980), p. 48.

Bohm describes the implicate order as a stream. He writes:

> On this stream, one may see an ever-changing pattern of vortices, ripples, waves, splashes, etc., which evidently have no independent existence as such. Rather, they are abstracted from the flowing movement, arising and vanishing in the total process of the flow. Such transitory subsistence as may be possessed by these abstracted forms implies only a relative independence or autonomy of behavior, rather than absolutely independent existence as ultimate substances.

6. For many examples, see Manley P. Hall, *The Secret Teachings of All Ages: An Encyclopedic Outline of Masonic, Hermetic, Qabbalistic and Rosicrucian Symbolic Philosophy. Being an Interpretation of the Secret Teachings Concealed within the Rituals, Allegories, and Mysteries of All Ages* (Los Angeles: The Philosophical Research Society, 1988), pp. 117–28.

7. Montague Ullman, "Dreams, Species-Connectedness, and the Paranormal," *The Journal of the American Society for Psychical Research* 84, no. 2 (April 1990).

8. Montague Ullman and Stanley Krippner with Alan Vaughan, *Dream Telepathy: Experiments in Nocturnal ESP* (New York: Macmillan, 1973; reprint, Jefferson, NC: McFarland & Co, 1989). Also see Montague Ullman, "Dreams, Species-Connectedness, and the Paranormal," *The Journal of the American Society for Psychical Research* 84, no. 2 (April 1990).

9. It is perhaps surprising that although some attention has been paid to telepathic dreams, little of the data so patiently accumulated over a period of twelve years has reached mainstream psychology. Much of this work was placed on solid scientific ground when Dr. Stanley Krippner and Charles Honorton joined the research effort originally proposed by Dr. Ullman when he was the director of dream research at Maimonides Medical Center in Brooklyn, New York.

Dr. Krippner was chiefly responsible for producing the quantitative experiments that the team accomplished over the twelve year period.

Altogether the team did twelve formal experiments in which nine were statistically significant. In the revised edition of their book (see endnote 8 above), Ullman et al. included an article by Dr. Irvin Child who analyzed all of the critical reports in the literature of their results showing that they indeed had valid evidence for telepathy in dreams.

10. An interesting and recent example of this dream phenomenon is illustrated in the bin Laden videotape discovered in December of 2001. In "Banality of bin Laden," *Time* (December 13, 2001), an online article dealing with the bin Laden video tape (http://www.time.com/time/nation/article/0,8599,188329,00.html), James Poniewozik reports that repeatedly bin Laden and the sheik with whom he's talking "talk about visions and dreams that associates had, before the attack, about planes crashing into buildings. This, perhaps, is something that Americans do not yet fully appreciate: these people live in another millennium, another mental universe."

CHAPTER 4
A Trickster in Our Memory

1. See "Memory (psychology)," Microsoft® Encarta® Online Encyclopedia 2001, http://encarta.msn.com.

A recent television program concerning the execution of the Oklahoma Federal building bomber, Timothy McVeigh, indicated that one witness recalled seeing a second person with McVeigh who really wasn't there at all! It seems that the witness was actually recalling events where he had met another man on a previous day and had put the two men together as one event.

2. See Julian Paul Keenan, Aaron Nelson, Margaret O'Connor, and Alvaro Pascual-Leone, "Neurology: Self-recognition and the Right Hemisphere," *Nature Brief Communication* 409 (January 18, 2001): p. 305. Also see " 'I' is to the Right, Neuroscientists Home in on the Bit of You that Knows You're You" in *Nature Science Update* (January 18, 2001) online at http://www.nature.com/nsu/010118/

010118-9.html. Keenan and his colleagues at Harvard Medical School in Boston studied patients who were having their brain hemispheres individually anaesthetized to investigate their epilepsy. While the left or right hemisphere was anaesthetized, the patients were shown photos of themselves morphed to blend their faces with that of a famous person, such as Marilyn Monroe. Afterwards, when asked to choose between a picture of themselves and a picture of the famous person, those whose right hemispheres had been anaesthetized thought they had been shown a photo of the famous person during anesthesia. If the left hemisphere had been anaesthetized the subject claimed that the photo they'd seen was of him- or herself.

Also see John Whitfield's article, "A Brain in Doubt Leaves It Out," *Nature Science Update*, online at http://www.nature.com/nsu/010614/010614-9.html. Whitfield reports that Yoram Bonneh, of the Smith-Kettlewell Eye Research Institute in San Francisco, and colleagues have shown that this behavior confirms the idea that activity in one half of the brain usually eclipses that in the opposite half. The brain seems to have internal theories about what the world is like. It then uses sensory input—which tends to be patchy and disorganized—to choose between these. In some sensory situations, different theories come into conflict, sending our perceptions awry.

Perhaps these experiments have more to say about the origin of schizophrenia and multiple personality syndrome than the researchers suspect. In such cases, it just may be that the appearance of dominance vanishes or switches unexpectedly.

3. According to the usual, or Bohr, interpretation of quantum physics, the quantum wave function "pops," changing from a field of possibilities to a single actuality when an observation occurs.

4. Remember what this means: you can't have both memory experiences at the same time. Thus arises the conflict between the egoic-self memory on a single layer and the soul memory encompassing them all. Perhaps all conflicts between soul- and self-dominant figures occur here. Perhaps this is how the mind-body duality arises.

5. For those of you curious about the mathematics, a sequence of 5 heads and 5 tails can occur in 252 different ways [10!/(5! × 5!)], while a sequence of 8 heads and 2 tails can occur in 45 ways [10!/(2! × 8!)]. If we also add the 210 sequences with 6 heads and 4 tails

$[10!/(6! \times 4!)]$ plus 210 sequences of 4 heads and 6 tails, we find that in addition to the 252 equal heads and tails we have a total of 672 sequences of roughly equal heads and tails, as compared to only 90 sequences with either 2 heads and 8 tails or 2 tails and 8 heads.

6. Karl H. Pribram, *Languages of the Brain: Experimental Paradoxes and Principles in Neuropsychology* (Monterey, CA: Brooks/Cole, 1977).

7. Ibid. I also described this experiment, briefly, in *Mind into Matter.*

8. Ibid.

9. Waves are wavy! They not only have amplitudes, or strengths, but also phases which indicate their oscillatory nature. To grasp this, think of the wave, when it arrives at a point of the film emulsion, as a pointer on a clock, say the second hand. If the wave has a large amplitude, it would correspond to a long pointer, and a wave with a small amplitude or strength would correspond to a small pointer. Now think of the number that the hand sweeps over as the phase of the wave at a given time. As the hand sweeps around the clock through sixty seconds, the phase of the wave advances a complete 360 degrees of the clock face marked by the hours.

10. Sigmund Freud, *New Introductory Lectures on Psychoanalysis,* standard edition, vol. 22 (New York: W. W. Norton, 1933, 1949), p. 74. The quote is continued in James Fadiman and Robert Frager's *Personality and Personal Growth* (New York: Harper & Row, 1976), p. 14: ". . . no recognition of the passage of time, and (a thing which is very remarkable and awaits adequate attention in philosophic thought) no alteration of mental processes by the passage of time. . . . Naturally the id knows no values, no good, no evil, no morality."

CHAPTER 5
The Curve of Life

1. A. Harry Klopf, *The Hedonistic Neuron: A Theory of Memory, Learning, and Intelligence* (Washington, DC: Hemisphere Publishing, 1982).

2. See endnote 5, chapter 4.

3. I am a great fan of English theater and plays. My favorite sneerer was the great actor Sir John Gielgud.

4. This just means that when you add up all of the possibilities you need to reach a probability of 1. For example, in the flip of a single coin you have two possibilities: heads with a probability of 50%, or not-heads with a probability of 50%. Add them up and you get 100% or 1.

5. A standard deviation provides a specific amount by which a value differs from the average. It is in essence a measure of the width of the bell-shaped curve.

6. If you are an experimental type, try taking 32 coins, any denomination, and putting them in a jar or can. Shake the can, throw the coins out on a table, and count heads. See how many times the number of heads falls within 16 plus or minus 3.

7. It may seem strange that 32 heads hardly ever shows up in this case. But with 32 coins being thrown, the sheer number of tosses practically guarantees that 1 of the 32 coins will be tails, even though the odds are small.

8. The well-known experiment involving pesticides or antibiotics comes to the fore here. When we take an antibiotic, it knocks out nearly every biological cell infecting the body. A few survive, however, resistant to the agent. Consequently, when these resistant strains multiply, the antibiotic agent is no longer effective. Many of the bacteria that were killed by the agent are no longer present. By not taking the antibiotic for a period of time, these nonresistant strains can reappear competing with the resistant strain. When the antibiotic is then taken again, it again knocks out the nonresistant strains. Hence a cycle of antibiotics, on and off, may be more effective in treatment than a continued, prolonged dosage.

CHAPTER 6
Sex: Information Flowing
Backward from the Future

1. Hoimar von Ditfurth, *The Origins of Life: Evolution as Creation*, trans. Peter Heinegg (San Francisco: Harper & Row, 1982).

2. Ibid.

3. See J. Lederberg and E. M. Lederberg. "Replica Plating and Indirect Selection of Bacterial Mutants." *Journal of Bacteriology* 63, no. 3 (March 1952): 399–406. According to a report found online at http://profiles.nlm.nih.gov/BB/Views/Exhibit/narrative/bacgen.html:

> Lederberg's work, which formed the basis for his Ph.D. dissertation, demonstrated that bacteria can in fact reproduce through sexual recombination, and opened up the genetics of microorganisms to the traditional methods of the field. These methods are central to the conduct of biotechnology and genetic engineering, an industry to which Lederberg has been a consultant since its inception.
>
> Lederberg's name is now mentioned in most textbooks of genetics and microbiology not only for his demonstration of bacterial conjugation, but also for his discovery (with Norton D. Zinder) of transduction (a virus-mediated form of bacterial genetic recombination); for coining the term plasmid to denote extra-chromosomal genetic material; and for his development of the technique of replica plating. His productive investigations into bacterial genetics led to his winning the Nobel Prize at the age of 33, for the work he initiated at age 20.

CHAPTER 7
The Eye to the Universe

1. As discussed in chapter 1, the principle of uncertainty, also called the principle of indeterminism, reflects the inability to predict the future based on the past or based on the present. Known as the cornerstone of quantum physics, it provides an understanding of why the world appears to be made of events that cannot be connected in terms of cause and effect.

Also as discussed in chapter 1, the complementarity principle says that the physical universe can never be known independently of the observer's choices of what to observe. These choices fall into two distinct or complementary categories of observation. Observation and determination carried out using one category always preclude the possibility of simultaneously observing and determining the complementary category. For example, the position of an object and the path it follows through space and time (the object's momentum) are observations in complementary categories and so cannot be determined simultaneously.

2. Note to computer programmers: This substitution is much like one found in a computer language code that says replace x by $1/(1 + x)$.

CHAPTER 9
The Structure of Love in the Universe

1. Carlo Suarès, *The Qabala Trilogy* (Boston, MA: Shambhala, 1985), pp. 274–75.

2. Ibid.

3. Paramahansa Yogananda, *Autobiography of a Yogi* (Los Angeles: Self-Realization Fellowship, 1973).

4. See my book *The Spiritual Universe: One Physicist's Vision of Spirit, Soul, Matter, and Self* (Portsmouth, NH: Moment Point Press, 1999), especially chapter 12.

BIBLIOGRAPHY

Aharonov, Yakir, Peter G. Bergmann, and Joel L. Lebowitz. "Time Symmetry in the Quantum Process of Measurement." *Physical Review* 134B (1964): 1410–16.

Albert, David Z. "On Quantum-Mechanical Automata." *Physics Letters* 98A, nos. 5, 6 (October 24, 1983): 249–52.

———. "How to Take a Photograph of Another Everett World." In *New Techniques and Ideas in Quantum Measurement Theory*, edited by D. M. Greenberger. Annals of the New York Academy of Sciences 480 (December 30, 1986).

Bohm, David. *Quantum Theory*. 1951. Reprint, New York: Dover Publications, 1989.

———. *Wholeness and the Implicate Order*. London, Boston: Routledge, 1980.

Bonneh, Y. S., A. Cooperman, and D. Sagi. "Motion-induced Blindness in Normal Observers." *Nature* 411 (2001): 798–801.

Corbin, Henri. *Mundis Imaginalis or the Imaginal and the Imaginary*. Ipswich, England: Golgonooza Press, 1972.

Crick, Francis. *The Astonishing Hypothesis: The Scientific Search for the Soul*. New York: Charles Scribner Sons, 1994.

Da Free John. *The Transcendence of Ego and Egoic Society*. Clearlake, CA: Johannine Daist Communion, 1982.

Darwin, Charles. *On the Origin of Species by Means of Natural Selection, or The Preservation of Favoured Races in the Struggle for Life*. London: John Murray, 1859.

Dawkins, Richard. *The Blind Watchmaker*. London: Longmans, 1986.

Dennett, Daniel G. *Darwin's Dangerous Idea: Evolution and the Meanings of Life*. New York: Touchstone Books, 1996.

Dewitt, Bryce S. "Quantum Mechanics and Reality." *Physics Today* (September 1970): 30–35.

Ditfurth, Hoimar von. *The Origins of Life: Evolution as Creation.* Translated by Peter Heinegg, San Francisco: Harper & Row, 1982.

Edinger, Edward F. *Anatomy of the Psyche: Alchemical Symbolism in Psychotherapy.* Chicago: Open Court, 1985.

Einstein, Albert. *Ideas and Opinions.* New York: Crown, 1954.

———. *The World As I See It.* Secaucus, NJ: Carol Publishing Group, 1999.

Einstein, A., R. C. Tolman, and B. Podolsky. "Knowledge of Past and Future in Quantum Mechanics." *Physics Review* 37 (1931): 780–81.

Eldridge, Niles. *Reinventing Darwin: The Great Debate at the High Table of Evolutionary Theory.* New York: John Wiley, 1995.

Ellis, Jean A. *From the Dreamtime: Australian Aboriginal Legends.* Australia: Collins Dove, 1991.

Fadiman, James, and Robert Frager. *Personality and Personal Growth.* New York: Harper & Row, 1976.

Freud, Sigmund. *New Introductory Lectures on Psychoanalysis.* Standard edition, vol. 22. New York: W. W. Norton, 1933, 1949.

———. *An Outline of Psychoanalysis.* Standard edition, vol. 23. New York: W. W. Norton, 1940.

———. *The Ego and the Id.* New York: W. W. Norton, 1960.

Gilchrist, Cherry. *The Elements of Alchemy.* Rockport, MA: Element, 1991.

Goswami, Amit. *The Self-Aware Universe: How Consciousness Creates the Material World.* New York: Tarcher/Putnam, 1993.

Hall, Manley P. *The Secret Teachings of All Ages: An Encyclopedic Outline of Masonic, Hermetic, Qabbalistic and Rosicrucian Symbolic Philosophy. Being an Interpretation of the Secret Teachings Concealed within the Rituals, Allegories, and Mysteries of All Ages.* Los Angeles: The Philosophical Research Society, 1988.

Hau, Lene Vestergaard. "Frozen Light." *Scientific American* (July 2001).

Heisenberg, Werner. *Physics and Philosophy.* New York: Harper & Row, 1958.

———. *Across the Frontier.* Woodbridge, CT: Oxbow Press, 1990.

Herbert, Nick. *Quantum Reality.* New York: Doubleday, 1985.

Hesse, Hermann, *Siddhartha.* Translated by Hilda Rossner. New York: New Directions, 1951.

Hobson, J. Allan. *The Dreaming Brain: How the Brain Creates Both the Sense and the Nonsense of Dreams.* New York: Basic Books, 1988.

Holmyard, E. J. *Alchemy.* New York: Dover, 1990.

Hoyle, Fred. *The Intelligent Universe.* New York: Holt, Rinehart, & Winston, 1983.

Jones, Shirley, editor. *The Mind of God and Other Musings: The Wisdom of Science.* San Rafael, CA: New World Library, 1994.

Kauffman, Stuart. *At Home in the Universe: The Search for Laws of Self-Organization and Complexity.* New York: Oxford University Press, 1995.

Keenan, Julian Paul, Aaron Nelson, Margaret O'Connor, and Alvaro Pascual-Leone. "Neurology: Self-recognition and the Right Hemisphere." *Nature Brief Communication* 409 (January 18, 2001): 305.

Keller, Evelyn Fox. *Refiguring Life: Metaphors of Twentieth-Century Biology.* New York: Columbia University Press, 1995.

Klopf, A. Harry. *The Hedonistic Neuron: A Theory of Memory, Learning, and Intelligence.* Washington, DC: Hemisphere Publishing, 1982.

Krishnamurti, J. and David Bohm. *The Ending of Time.* San Francisco: HarperSanFrancisco, 1985.

Jung, C. G. *Analytical Psychology: Its Theory & Practice.* New York: Vintage, 1970.

Klossowski de Rola, Stanislas. *Alchemy: The Secret Art.* New York: Thames & Hudson, 1973, 1997.

Lederberg, J. and E. M. Lederberg. "Replica Plating and Indirect Selection of Bacterial Mutants." *Journal of Bacteriology* 63 (1952): 399.

Levi, Eliphas. *Transcendental Magic.* Chicago, 1910. This work was quoted in Stanislas Klossowski de Rola. *Alchemy: The Secret Art.* New York: Thames & Hudson, 1973, 1997.

Libet, B. E., W. Wright, B. Feinstein, and Dennis Pearl. "Subjective Referral of the Timing for a Conscious Sensory Experience: A Functional Role for the Somatosensory Specific Projection System in Man." *Brain* 102, part 1 (March 1979).

Lwoff, André. *Biological Order.* Cambridge, MA: MIT Press, 1962.

McLuhan, Marshall. *The Medium is the Massage: An Inventory of Effects.* San Francisco: Hardwired, 1996.

Mindell, Arnold. *Dreambody: The Body's Role in Revealing the Self.* Santa Monica, CA: Sigo Press, 1982.

Pauli, Wolfgang. "Ideas of the Unconscious from the Standpoint of Natural Science and Epistemology." *Dialectica* 8, no. 4 (December 1954).

————. "Science and Western Thought." In *Europa: Erbe und Auftrag,* edited by M. Gohring. Mainz, Germany: Internationaler Gelehrtenkongress, 1955.

————. Letter to C. G. Jung (March 1953). Exhibited in the Pauli Room at CERN, Geneva.

Pouley, Jim. *The Secret of Dreaming.* Australia, Templestowe: Red Hen, 1988.

Pribram, Karl H. *Languages of the Brain: Experimental Paradoxes and Principles in Neuropsychology.* Monterey, CA: Brooks/Cole, 1977.

Price, Huw. *Time's Arrow and Archimedes' Point.* New York: Oxford University Press, 1996.

Regardie, Israel. *The Golden Dawn.* St. Paul, MN: Llewellyn, 1989.

Roberts, Jane. *The Unknown Reality.* Vol 1. Englewood Cliffs, NJ: Prentice-Hall, 1977. Reprint, San Rafael, CA: Amber-Allen, 1996.

Rosen, Eliot Jay, editor. *Experiencing the Soul: Before Birth, During Life, After Death.* Carlsbad, CA: Hay House, 1998.

Schiff, Leonard I. *Quantum Mechanics.* 3rd ed. New York: McGraw-Hill, 1955, 1968.

Scholem, Gershom. *Major Trends in Jewish Mysticism.* New York: Schocken Books, 1974.

Schrödinger, Erwin. *My View of the World.* Cambridge, England: Cambridge University Press, 1964. Reprint, Woodbridge, CT: Ox Box Press, 1983. Originally published in German (Hamburg-Vienna: Paul Zsolnay Verlag, 1961).

————. *What is Life? & Mind and Matter.* Cambridge, England: Cambridge University Press, 1967.

Smoley, Richard. "My Mind Plays Tricks on Me." *Gnosis* (spring 1991): 12.

Suarès, Carlo. *The Cipher of Genesis: The Original Code of the Qabala as Applied to the Scriptures.* Berkeley, CA: Shambhala, 1970.

————. "The Cipher of Genesis." In *Tree 2: Yetzirah*, edited by David Meltzer. Santa Barbara, CA: Christopher Books, 1971. From a lecture by Suarès reprinted from *Systematics* 8, no. 2 (September 1970).

————. *Les Spectrogrammes de l'Alphabet Hebraïque.* Geneva, Switzerland: Mont-Blanc, 1973.

————. *The Qabala Trilogy.* Boston, MA: Shambhala, 1985.

————. *The Second Coming of Reb Yhshwh.* York, ME: Samuel Weiser, 1994.

Sutton, Peter, editor. *Dreamings: The Art of Aboriginal Australia.* Australia, Victoria: Penguin, 1988.

Ullman, Montague. "Dreaming, Altered States of Consciousness, and the Problem of Vigilance." In *The Journal of Nervous and Mental Disease* 133, no. 6 (December 1961).

————. "Wholeness and Dreaming." In B. J. Hiley and F. D. Peat, editors, *Quantum Implications: Essays in Honor of David Bohm* (London: Routledge & Kegan Paul, 1987): 386–95.

————. "Dreams, Species-Connectedness, and the Paranormal." In *The Journal of the American Society for Psychical Research* 84, no. 2 (April 1990).

————. "Dream, Metaphor and Psi." Unpublished manuscript.

Ullman, Montague, Stanley Krippner, and Alan Vaughan. *Dream Telepathy: Experiments in Nocturnal ESP.* New York: Macmillan, 1973. Revised, Jefferson, NC and London: McFarland, 1989.

Ullman, Montague and Nan Zimmerman. *Working with Dreams: Self-understanding, Problem-solving, and Enriched Creativity through Dream Appreciation.* Los Angeles: J. P. Tarcher, 1979.

Vaidman, Lev. "Time-Symmetrized Counterfactuals in Quantum Theory." Online at http://xxx.lanl.gov/ (quant-ph/9807075, July 27, 1998).

von Békésy, Georg. *Sensory Inhibition.* Princeton, NJ: Princeton University Press, 1967.

von Franz, Marie-Louise. *Number and Time: Reflections Leading to a Unification of Depth Psychology and Physics.* Evanston, IL: Northwestern University Press, 1974.

————. *Alchemical Active Imagination*. Boston, MA: Shambhala, 1997.

Walker, Barbara G. *The Woman's Encyclopedia of Myths and Secrets*. New York: Harper & Row, 1983.

Waterson, Robert and John Sulston. "Genome Sequence of the Nematode *C. Elegans*: A Platform for Investigating Biology." *Science* 282 (1998): pp. 2012–21.

Watzlawick, Paul. *How Real Is Real?* New York: Random House, 1976.

Weiner, Norbert. *God & Golem, Inc.: A Comment on Certain Points Where Cybernetics Impinges on Religion*. Cambridge, MA: MIT Press, 1964.

Wheeler, John Archibald. "How Come the Quantum?" in *New Techniques and Ideas in Quantum Measurement Theory*, edited by D. M. Greenberger. Annals of the New York Academy of Sciences 408 (December 30, 1986).

————. "Information, Physics, Quantum: The Search for Links." In *Complexity, Entropy, and the Physics of Information*. Santa Fe Institute Studies in the Sciences of Complexity 8, edited by W. H. Zurich. Redwood City, CA: Addison-Wesley, 1990.

Winson, Jonathan. *Brain and Psyche*. New York: Anchor Press/Doubleday, 1985.

————."The Meaning of Dreams." *Scientific American* (November 1990).

Wolf, Fred Alan. *Taking the Quantum Leap: The New Physics for Nonscientists*. San Francisco: Harper & Row, 1981. Revised, New York: HarperCollins, 1989.

————. *Star Wave: Mind, Consciousness, and Quantum Physics*. New York: Macmillan, 1984.

————. "The Quantum Physics of Consciousness: Toward a New Psychology," *Integrative Psychology* 3 (1985): 236–47.

————. *The Body Quantum: The New Physics of Body, Mind, and Health*. New York: Macmillan, 1986.

————. "The Physics of Dream Consciousness: Is the Lucid Dream a Parallel Universe?" *Lucidity Letter* 6, no. 2 (December 1987): 130–35.

————. *Parallel Universes: The Search for Other Worlds*. New York: Simon & Schuster, 1989.

————. "On the Quantum Physical Theory of Subjective Antedating." In *Journal of Theoretical Biology* 136 (1989): 13–19.

————. *The Eagle's Quest: A Physicist's Search for Truth in the Heart of the Shamanic World.* New York: Summit, 1991.

————. "The Dreaming Universe." *Gnosis* 22 (winter 1992): 30–35.

————. *The Dreaming Universe: A Mind-expanding Journey into the Realm Where Psyche and Physics Meet.* New York: Simon & Schuster, 1994. Reprint, New York: Touchstone, 1995.

————. "The Body in Mind." *Psychological Perspectives: A Journal of Global Consciousness Integrating Psyche, Soul and Nature* 30 (fall–winter 1994): 22–35.

————. "The Quantum Mechanics of Dreams and the Emergence of Self-Awareness." In *Toward a Scientific Basis for Consciousness*, edited by S. R. Hameroff, A. W. Kaszniak, and A. C. Scott. Boston, MA: MIT Press, 1996.

————. "The Soul and Quantum Physics." In *Experiencing the Soul: Before Birth, During Life, After Death*, edited by Eliot Jay Rosen. Carlsbad, CA: Hay House, 1998: 245–52.

————. "The Timing of Conscious Experience." In *Journal of Scientific Exploration* 12, no. 4 (winter 1998): 511–42.

————. "A Quantum Physics Model of the Timing of Conscious Experience." In *Toward a Science of Consciousness III*, edited by Stuart Hameroff, Al Kaszniak, and David Chalmers. Cambridge, MA: MIT Press, 1999: 359–66.

————. "The Quantum Physical Communication Between the Self and the Soul." In *Noetic Journal* 2, no. 2 (April 1999).

————. *The Spiritual Universe: One Physicist's Vision of Spirit, Soul, Matter, and Self.* Portsmouth, NH: Moment Point Press, 1999. Originally published as *The Spiritual Universe: How Quantum Physics Proves the Existence of the Soul.* New York: Simon & Schuster, 1996.

————. *Mind into Matter: A New Alchemy of Science and Spirit.* Portsmouth, NH: Moment Point Press, 2001.

Yogananda, Paramahansa. *Autobiography of a Yogi.* Los Angeles: Self-Realization Fellowship, 1973.

Zohar: The Book of Enlightenment. Translation and introduction by Daniel Chanan Matt. Mahwah, New Jersey: Paulist Press, 1983.

INDEX

ABOUT THE AUTHOR

National Book Award winner Dr. Fred Alan Wolf is a consulting physicist and the author of ten books. He earned his Ph.D. in theoretical physics from UCLA and has taught at San Diego State University, the University of London, the University of Paris, the Hahn-Meitner Institute for Nuclear Physics in Berlin, and the Hebrew University of Jerusalem. He is also a member of the Martin Luther King, Jr. Collegium of Scholars. He lives in San Francisco with his wife Sonia.

To contact Dr. Wolf, please write c/o Moment Point Press, PO Box 4549, Portsmouth, NH 03802, or email him at wolf@momentpoint.com. Visit his web page at http://home.ix.netcom.com/~fawolf and at www.momentpoint.com.

OTHER BOOKS OF INTEREST FROM
MOMENT POINT PRESS

Mind into Matter
a new alchemy
of science and spirit
Fred Alan Wolf, Ph.D.

The Spiritual Universe
one physicist's vision of
spirit, soul, matter, and self
Fred Alan Wolf, Ph.D.

Lessons from the Light
what we can learn from
the near-death experience
Kenneth Ring, Ph.D.

The God of Jane
a psychic manifesto
Jane Roberts
a Classics in Consciousness
series book

Consciously Creating Each Day
a 365-day perpetual calendar of
spirited thought
from voices past and present
Susan Ray, Editor

for more information
visit us at
www.momentpoint.com